GLEANINGS FROM
THE DIARY AND MINISTRY OF
JAMES MORRISON

# GLEANINGS

# FROM

# THE DIARY AND MINISTRY

# OF

# JAMES MORRISON

by

G. N. M. Collins

First published 1984

© 

G. N. M. Collins

Printed by Lindsay & Co. Ltd., Edinburgh

# FOREWORD

We are indebted to Professor Collins for undertaking this work. His skill as a writer, combined with the authority of the historian, and his intimate knowledge of Mr Morrison, are clearly reflected in his handling of the diaries. He has skilfully selected from them, the material which faithfully represents Mr Morrison, and at the same time is not unjust to those who did not always agree with him. To achieve this, he has maintained a delicate poise throughout. The background to many of the events referred to has been graphically and succinctly sketched as would be expected from an accomplished writer. This will help the reader who is unfamiliar with certain events, places, customs and people referred to in the book.

We trust that the Lord will bless this book, and that the reader will be stirred to emulate the faithfulness, courage and resourcefulness of the humble servant of Christ, and able student of the Word, that Mr Morrison undoubtedly was.

He has finished his course. The storm has changed into an endless calm and the desired haven has been reached where "They shall hunger no more, neither thirst any more; neither shall the sun light on them, nor any heat. For the Lamb which is in the midst of the throne shall feed them and lead them unto living fountains of waters: and God shall wipe away all tears from their eyes." (Rev. 7: 17).

JOHN MORRISON.

# INTRODUCTION

What James Morrison's purpose was in writing a diary does not become fully evident in anything that he has written. The diary itself begins in 1964 and ends with an entry dated 8th April 1982, thus covering only the last 18 years of his long ministry in North Uist; but the memories of events in earlier years which he has brought into the narrative help us to form a clearer picture of the man himself and a fuller understanding of the influences which shaped his youth.

Altogether, the diary reads like a book of remembrance compiled mainly for personal use. It is pervaded by a spirit of gratitude and thanksgiving, and the writer is obviously moved by the same desire as led the Psalmist to write, "Bless the Lord, O my soul, and forget not all His benefits".

There is, however, a hint of putting it to a more public use in an entry dated 31st March 1980. He had been reading the diary of his friend, Rev. Kenneth A. Macrae of Stornoway, and expressing his appreciation of what he had disclosed of his spiritual life in those jottings. And then he adds, "For a number of years I have been interested in the maintenance of a record of my own life. Already I have written much, but in the main I just penned it all as things happened without ever leaving many names out of it that *should* have been left out. If the Lord spares me to retire, and I have my powers . . . I should be glad to erase many things from this record altogether."

This hint of intention to publish is confirmed by his cousin, the Rev. John Morrison of Fort William, who informs us that Rev. James Morrison actually discussed the publication of the diaries with him.

At all events, it is quite clear that the diarist realised the need of purgative revision if what he had written was to be given a more permanent form. With the concurrence, therefore, of Mrs Morrison, and the Rev. John Morrison, I have proceeded on this plan, fitting the diary extracts into a framework of biography, thereby making the whole narrative as autobiographical as possible.

James Morrison would have squirmed with embarrassment if anyone had ever suggested that he bore a likeness to Samuel Rutherford; yet the likeness was there. "I am a man of extremes" was how Rutherford described himself to David Dickson, and in that, at least, James Morrison resembled him. Both men had hot tempers and could, while in the mood, like Dandie Dinmont's terrier, "behave themselves *distinctly*". Rutherford, according to one of his students was "of such a bizarre temper that his very beard pricked up to his lips". And, providing the beard, the same could be said of Morrison! But it was true of them both that "e'en their failings leaned to virtue's side". Rutherford's polemics were rooted in love to Christ and concern for his cause, and it is no extravagance to claim the same for the obscure pastor of the Free Church in North Uist. "Mr Morrison has many enemies in North Uist," remarked a critic to Rev. K. A. MacRae of Stornoway. "Yes," came the quick rejoinder, "and many friends too." It all depended on the view-point!

The more winsome side of Rutherford's nature is brought out in his incomparable letters, letters that he never expected to be published. And it is with a view to bringing to light the other side of James Morrison's character that we publish these extracts from the diary in which, at the end of each day, he called himself to judgment. Perhaps, as we read, we shall be moved to kneel beside him and make *our* penitent appeal to the everlasting mercy of our Sovereign God.

G. N. M. COLLINS.

*Edinburgh, July 1984.*

# CONTENTS

# CHAPTER ONE

# THE EARLY YEARS

My boast is not that I deduce my birth
From loins enthroned, and rulers of the earth,
But higher far my proud pretensions rise, —
The son of parents passed into the skies.
                              —COWPER.

James Morrison's training for the ministry of the Gospel
began long before he became aware of a call to the service of
Christ and His Church. Brought up in Scalpay, a small
island off the mainland of Harris, he was reared in a
community where religion moulded the lives of the people,
and where godly men and women lived out their days in a
climate of sincere and simple piety — straitened indeed in
material circumstances, yet rich in faith and remarkably
contented with their lot, knowing that there is stored up, for
all who fear the Lord, "an inheritance, incorruptible, and
undefiled, and that fadeth not away, reserved in heaven"
for the heirs of salvation.

— 1 —

Ecclesiastically, the attachment of the Scalpay people had
been to the Free Church of Scotland since the Disruption of
1843. The spiritual revival which had accompanied that
historic event had spread to many parts of the Western Isles.
The reign of Moderatism was broken and, once more, the
re-vitalising power of the Spirit was in evidence. As at
Pentecost, so now, the Lord was adding to the Church daily
such as were being saved.

It mattered little to these good island folk that, in the
course of the years, as it drew near to the end of the century,
the teaching of the Church's Colleges had become tainted
with the Rationalism that had taken over in several

theological schools on the Continent; the sounds of battle were too distant and, indeed, too muted, to cause alarm, and when proposals of Union between the Free Church of Scotland and the United Presbyterian Church were made, they caused relatively little disquiet in the Western Isles. After all, there were no United Presbyterians on the scene, and they were constantly being assured by the advocates of Union that such an event, if it materialised, would make absolutely no difference to them. Both Churches, it was averred, held by the Westminster Confession of Faith, and therefore the way to Union was clear and open. Such points of difference as remained, especially the Establishment Principle defining the relations of Church and State, were so insignificant they could well be treated as "open questions".

It was not yet generally appreciated that a Declaratory Act, passed by a large majority vote in the Free Church General Assembly in 1892 was really a relieving Act, with the effect of giving ordinands the opportunity to relax their acceptance of the Church's historic standards without risking their position as ordinands of the Free Church of Scotland. Such an Act was also part of the price required from the Free Church for the privilege of uniting with the United Presbyterian Church, which already had an Act of this nature on its statute-book.

But all this meant very little to the good people of Scalpay. No note of heresy was heard from the pulpits of Harris, and they simply followed their ministers into the United Free Church which came into being in 1900, assured that all things remained as they were. And, judging by the local scene, so they did.

But some had their misgivings. The Free Presbyterian secession of 1893 had, at least, revealed that the recent Union had not been brought about without loss of identity by the large section of the former Free Church which had entered into it. Furthermore, the continued existence of the Free Church of Scotland in the minority who had declined to enter the Union of 1900 raised doubts in the minds of the Scalpay people as to the ingenuousness of some of the advocates of union whose lead they had followed. The name of Dr John Kennedy of Dingwall was still influential in the Highlands, and he had been opposed to union when the matter was first mooted many years before. Not that he was against union as such, but he was inflexibly opposed to an ecclesiastical merger that required the blurring of vital distinctions to bring it about. In a pamphlet which he had written on the subject, he addressed this admonition to the compromising pro-union majority, "Of one thing be assured, that, of your ministers, elders, deacons, and people, not a few are resolved, not to forsake the banner of the Free Church, and are resolved too, not to separate from you, till you have parted from them, by being actually incorporated with those whose fellowship you have preferred. They will adhere to you as long as they can, and if there be a disruption, the act shall be yours, and all Christendom shall know that it is."

— 2 —

The Constitutionalists of 1900, greatly diminished since Kennedy's time, had followed through his plan of resistance. Their case had gone by appeal to the House of Lords, and that august tribunal had declared in their favour. The minority who had declined to enter the Union were declared to be the true Free Church of Scotland as they had always claimed, whereas their former brethren, who had tried to disinherit them, were firmly told that they had disinherited themselves.

These events had the result of alerting the people at last to the theological changes which were taking place in the Colleges of the Church. The Declaratory Act of 1892 had become a kind of "Heretic's Charter". Professor Robertson Smith had been removed from his College Chair in Aberdeen, because of heresy, before this measure became operative, but after 1900 the way of the heretical innovater was made safe. Charges of unsound teaching were indeed made, from time to time, against certain Professors and Ministers; but, under the new legislation, they found adequate protection from the Church's discipline.

Many throughout the Church, who had entered the

United Free Church in good faith were now becoming uneasy. A still wider Union was in prospect, and it soon became evident that further sweeping changes would have to be made if this more comprehensive amalgamation was to be achieved. When, in fact, it was achieved, in 1929, several former Free Church people who had become United Free in 1900, now returned to their former allegiance. In November 1929, the United Free congregation of Scalpay was received back into the Free Church of Scotland, and, in 1933, the Rev. D. G. Ferguson was inducted as their first independent minister, for in earlier years they had been just a mission station under Tarbert.

Under the enthusiastic leadership of Mr Roderick Cunningham — a local ship-owner and merchant — the newly-sanctioned congregation set about putting its house in order. The old church building was demolished, and a new one was erected near its site. Mr Cunningham brought the building material, free of charge, to the island, and it was man-handled from the ship to the site by enthusiastic helpers — women and even children playing their own part. Nehemiah's account of the work of restoration in Jerusalem might be applied to the situation in Scalpay in those days; "So built we the wall; and all the wall was joined together unto the half thereof: *for the people had a mind to work*" (Nehemiah 4: 6).

Within a few years, Scalpay was sending a succession of young men into the Free Church College to be trained for the ministry of the Free Church. Among them was James Morrison.

— 3 —

Born in 1910, James had spent his early life in Scalpay. A keen-minded and quick-witted youth, he had taken full advantage of the educational facilities that were available in his island home, but with no thought of pursuing his schooling to higher levels. The sea was in his blood. His father was an expert fisherman and handler of boats, and James's highest ambition was to be a fisherman too, and to skipper a boat of his own. But the same Lord Who had, in

His early ministry, called away another James from his boat and nets was soon to address the same compelling call to James Morrison, "Follow Me, and I will make you a fisher of men".

Precisely by what means James Morrison was brought into a saving experience of the Gospel does not appear to be known even to his most intimate friends. He was undoubtedly a child of the covenant, the son of godly parents who spared no pains to bring up their family "in the nurture and admonition of the Lord", and who consistently exemplified in their own dedicated lives the Gospel which they so firmly believed, and which they desired their children to share with them.

James always had a photograph of his parents set up in a place of prominence in his home, where he would have to pass it several times in the course of the day. To him, it was a "speaking likeness" in more than the accepted sense of the phrase. It is germane to our purpose to note how he refers to it in his diary in after years.

"Every time I pass, especially in recent years, the photograph of my parents, with myself and Bella as children included in it, as it stands on a table on our first landing, I feel constrained both to thank God for such parents, and to breathe a prayer to make me worthy of them. And I often think of my parents as the personification of wholeness. A neighbour, a Christian lady, once commended my father to her husband thus: 'No one is without some weakness, but, as I look on John, I do not know where to find one'."

— 4 —

Nothing ever weakened his bond with the old home in Scalpay. Writing in 1966 during a visit there he notes:

"27th January: Dear old Bayhead had a warm welcome for me. Sisters Johan and Chirstag were there to greet me. They had a lovely table spread for me and a blazing fire. Afterwards, Chirstag wanted me to sleep in her home, but I preferred to do so in the old home. And the poor dog, 'Bunty' preferred that too! How that touched me! What fine things are in nature if we had the proper attitude to

5

them! God was with me this day, of a truth. I loved to open the Book where my worthy parents lived and loved to the end."

Another entry runs:

"1st February 1966: No place in the world that I know is to be compared with Scalpay. The worthy men and women who have graced it in its distant past have worthy successors there still. God grant that this will continue to the end of time. I love the very dust of it. How the little brook that runs down at the front speaks to me! It seems to call me back to days and nights of years gone by. Voices that were a joy to hear are now silent in the grave. But we look for a new heaven and a new earth."

A visit in 1978 produced the following entry:

"5th September: In dear old Bayhead. Worship had a few affecting moments for me, both last night and this morning. Here my dear and worthy parents lived and loved. Here dear auntie so often prayed; here dear Duncan (a brother) attained to manhood. Here he always greeted us with love and affection. I should feel much indebted to God that I have worthy sisters still left me here; also proved friends. Dear Finlay, across the road, our late Duncan's friend, was so thoughtful that he had the well cleaned for our home-coming. What history is bound up in that well! I loved a drink from it today. It will be my joy to drink from it every day that I am here."

A meeting with other members of the family, in his brother's Manse in Skye, gives rise to other thoughts of the old home.

"14th January: Last night we had a very solemn and soul-enriching worship. My dear sisters, Johan and Mary, were with us. I could not help thinking of my late dear father. How his prayers for his family seemed to have special significance last night! This appeared to me when we all, on bended knee, sought the Lord's blessing on us all! What great things God as done for us as a family! May it please Him to cover us always."

6

Scalpay Harbour (*see page 1*).

Workers together (see page 4).

There are frequent references in the diary to Norman, a younger brother, who also entered the ministry. In the basic elements of faith and conduct the two men were alike, but in most other respects the differences were distinct and striking. Norman was as marked by *suaviter in modo* as James was by *fortiter in re*. Norman's soft voice, quiet smile and ingratiating manner served him well in many a difficult situation. He was minister successively in Stoer and Duirinish, Skye, and he left his mark for good on both communities. James and he were bound together in the strongest bonds of brotherly affection, and Norman's death, in 1972, after a short illness, left James disconsolate. In his diary he lives again the trauma of those days.

"What made it so crushing," he recalls, "was that I never anticipated it." Not, indeed, until he reached Aberdeen, and had a talk with one of the surgeons in the Royal Infirmary there, did he realise that there was no hope of Norman's recovery. When he saw him the following day, however, they had a chat that James never forgot. "He talked to me freely," he writes, "and his shrewd common-sense was in action all the time. He wished me to advise his dear wife to think of a house in Inverness where she would be sure to be near the children, and where she would be likely to find some light work. He added, 'If it should please God to spare me for some time it would be in my interest to be there too, to be near medical help always'."

But there was to be no extension of time. The entry for 5th October 1972, records the end of Norman's pilgrimage: "This day, at 3.15 a.m. my dear brother Norman departed this life to be forever with the Lord." He was interred at Stoer, by his own wish, and laid to rest among the people whose call had brought him into his first charge as a minister of the Word.

"I found it sore to believe," concludes James, "that my dear Norman was no more available to me. . . . God grant me to translate all my pinings into prayer and praises, that all should be truly sanctified to me unto the end of my life here."

Duncan, the other brother, who remained in the old home in Scalpay, also predeceased James, and once again the diary strikes a plaintive note. "His end," writes James, "was indeed a tragic one. He had a few torches in the house, and any visitor who had reason to call, and who arrived without a torch, would be sure to leave in the darkness with one of Duncan's torches. Yet he himself was found dead with a box of matches in his hand, the indication being that he was lighting his way with their aid. . . . He had in mind visiting Finlay across the road. He slipped on the treacherous little bridge, and must have had so much concussion that, before he came round, the exposure was too much for him. So the Doctor said. I have no brother left now. The worship at night was blessed to me."

\*     \*     \*     \*

From the time of the death of John Morrison, James's father, the rest of the household seemed to look to James as his natural successor in the headship of the family, and the responsibility was affectionately accepted. They came to him with their problems and respected his counsels. A letter from a sister, written while she was in hospital, rejoiced his heart. "She had always been so reserved in relation to her spiritual life," he writes, "but, on this occasion, she shared part of her soul's breathings with me. She said: 'These words: *None perish that Him trust* were made very precious to me the day of my operation — and since then — and I felt very reconciled to the Lord's Will in all His dealings with me. And may that remain.' She further added: 'and may your prayers on my, and on our, behalf be blessed to us and to you at all times'. This touched me much, for ever since my worthy father was taken, I have solemnly felt that his priesthood has fallen on me in the name of the High Priest over the house — His own house. I have been taught of Him to bear — after Him — all my brothers and sisters and their children to the end of the world on my heart and on my shoulders always."

The old church in Scalpay to which John Morrison and his wife brought their children for public worship was still in use when the present writer paid his first visit to Scalpay in March 1936. It was communion time, but even the gale-force winds and hail showers were no deterrent to the zealous people who assembled to the services. The preachers had to compete with the noisy musketry of the warring elements, but the congregation, inured, no doubt to such conditions, refused to be distracted.

After the first service, as we made our way back to the Manse, a particularly wild shower broke upon us. Umbrellas were useless. A fierce wind peppered us with the largest hail-stones I had even seen. As we battled on, another minister and I, we overtook an old man who had been at the service. He was showing no signs of stress or strain, and his rubicund face wrinkled into a happy smile as we greeted him in the passing. But he was not done with us.

*"Nach sinn a fhuair an la math*?'' (Didn't we get a good day?) he cried above the storm.

*"Nach sinn a fhuair?"* (Isn't it we who did?) I echoed sympathetically.

My companion was aghast. "If this is what they call a 'good day' in Scalpay,'' he murmured, as we pulled away, "I shouldn't care to be here when it is really stormy.''

Later in the day, as we sat in the comfort of a glowing peat fire in the Manse study, we told Rev. D. G. Ferguson, who was by then minister of Scalpay, of our encounter on the way home.

"What was he like?'' asked Mr Ferguson, with reference to the old man of the story.

Our description must have been accurate, for the identification was immediate and positive.

"Ah,'' said our host, "that is one of the finest Christians in Scalpay. And he wasn't thinking of the weather. God had given him a 'good day' at the Gospel table.''

It was among such people that young James Morrison grew up, and their impress was upon him for the rest of his life.

9

# CHAPTER TWO

# COLLEGE DAYS

**A minister is not made without learning, but, O, learning does not make a minister.**
—LACHLAN MACKENZIE of Lochcarron.

To return to studies after an interval of several years must have been a daunting thought for James Morrison, but the challenge was taken up in the strong conviction that his call to the Gospel ministry was from God Himself. The difficulties of the coming years were assessed in that light. If this thing was of the Lord, then the Lord would provide. Financial aid for aspirants to higher education — especially for those who came into the category of "mature students", as they are now designated, was not generous, nor easily come by, and the resources of the churches were always under strain.

The situation necessitated that many students had to offer themselves for "pulpit supply" service during vacations, and even during the academic sessions. The system had its advantages and disadvantages, with the latter outweighing the former. It meant that the student's time for study was seriously curtailed, and that the general burden of work was increased to danger point. In addition, it sometimes had the effect of convincing the glib prattler that he had already mastered the art of preaching, and might therefore relax his application to general study.

On the side of advantage, the judicious student might devise a system of study whereby his preparation for the pulpit might be so dove-tailed into his more academic disciplines as to make both branches of learning mutually supportive and corrective. At the same time, the young preacher would have a practical training that would stand him in good stead in coming days. By force of circumstances, James had to plan his course along these lines.

Looking back, he saw the hand of God in it all. It had the effect of bringing him out of himself. The natural tendency of the remote isles-man is to become insular in outlook, and James was well aware of this risk. His ministry, in future years, was to be given to an island congregation, but that, as yet, was hidden in the providence of God. For the present, he must make the acquaintance of the Free Church of Scotland throughout her borders, and that, especially, was where his student-preaching came in. It took him to different parts of the country to meet with people of a different culture from that in which he had been reared. It widened his horizons, and made him aware of problems that he had never had to face in the Isles of the West. There were times, too, when he was sent to assist ministers for whom the work of the pastorate was becoming too heavy.

— 1 —

It was in this connection that he first made the acquaintance of the Rev. Angus Mackay, of Kingussie and Newtonmore. Mr Mackay was born in Canada, of Scottish parentage who were of the very best emigrant stock. He had come to the help of the church of his fathers after the debacle of 1900 and was immediately called to Kingussie, where he remained for the rest of his long life, a pastor affectionately regarded and highly revered. There James Morrison assisted him during one of his College vacations, and a warm friendship grew up between them. But there was one disturbing element. James was a smoker, as most young fishermen were in his time, and Mr Mackay classed smoking among the lusts of the flesh — an evil habit in which no Christian should indulge. But James remained unconvinced, and the bad habit retained its mastery. What could be done about it?

Mr Mackay decided that desperate diseases called for desperate remedies! He enlisted the support of the whole congregation! At the close of James's last service in Kingussie on that occasion, Mr Mackay paid generous tribute to his young helper. He was a good student, an attractive preacher, a winsome Christian, but *he smoked!*

And the minister called upon his congregation that they would join him in prayer for Mr Morrison that he might be delivered from this bad habit!

There was a sequel. Some years afterwards, Mr Morrison — now an ordained minister, was visiting his home island of Scalpay where he met, of all people, a young lady from Greece who was there on a short visit. They were not long in conversation when the visitor produced her cigarette-case, and lit up! James disapproved, and told her why. It was unseemly in *a lady* to smoke. But, unabashed, the lady smoked on, remarking laconically that what *she* would be more ready to regard as unseemly was that *a minister of the Gospel* should smoke! The shaft went home. James threw away his packet of cigarettes, vowing that he would never smoke again, and urging his fair remonstrant to take up the challenge with him.

Some of his friends teased James about it afterwards, saying that the young Athenian had succeeded where Mr Mackay had failed. But James would not have it. God had answered his old friend's prayer by means of this young lady who had shown him so effectively his blindness to his own faults, and his inconsistency in condemning in others what he so glibly excused in himself. It was God, he insisted, moving "in a mysterious way His wonders to perform".

Many years later he fell in with a man, a total stranger, who was attending a funeral in the island. "What a providence this was," he writes, as he recalls this chance encounter. "It started with a question about smoking. I was asked how I stopped it. When I completed my story he referred to a Greek lady journalist and added that that story was quoted in her book. I remembered meeting her and advising her against smoking; this was nearly twenty years ago. How wonderful are God's ways!"

And yet again, within a decade of his death, the incident came back to him. The reading at family worship one evening touched on the subject of "fuller and truer dedication to the Lord". Memories arose of that evening in 1951, "when I laid down my cigarettes and never took up a single one again".

So far so good; but there still remained "much land to be possessed". "Should I not" he asks, "deny myself in a similar way in every other area of my moral and spiritual life? Surely that is a sober and sensible reflection."

— 2 —

When, after obtaining his Arts degree, James entered the Free Church College, the changed climate was altogether to his liking. Here he sat at the feet of teachers who were wholly committed to the Reformed Faith. The professorial team was headed by Dr John Macleod, who also held the chair of Apologetics. Dr Donald Maclean was in Church History; Dr Kennedy Cameron in Systematic Theology; Dr P. W. Miller in Hebrew and Old Testament; and Dr Alexander Ross in Greek and New Testament. It was a matter of great satisfaction to him that two of the 1900 Constitutionalists, Dr Kennedy Cameron and Dr Donald Maclean, were still on the staff of the college when he was passing through. Years later, when he used, as a commissioner, to attend the General Assembly, he made it a habit to slip quietly into the classrooms of the College and give thanks to God for the blessings that he had received through the teaching of these men.

The following extracts from his diary speak for themselves.

"Before I found my way to the Assembly I was led to resolve to have prayer in all the classrooms in the College to thank God for the help I received in them; particularly that I was helped to read my Bible better, that is by giving me a relish for Greek and Hebrew. And I venture to think that I know both much better now than I did then. Today I had prayer alone in the Common Room. From there I proceeded to the Hebrew Room. I endeavoured to pray in the very place where I used to sit in past days. How God has covered me since those days! Holy is His name. I was happy with the Assembly's work today. God prosper all that He took pleasure in."

On other occasions he had company in these nostalgic sessions. One day he met in with an American student to whom he took an immediate liking. "This afternoon" he writes, "I had a sweet time with a young student from America; and we ended our converse with prayer in the Greek classroom. These are moments that have a healing virtue for us, and we know this to be so just as the dear woman of old knew in her own body that she was healed of her plague."

Later, he writes: "I asked William Macdowell of the Irish Evangelical Church to have prayer with me. We bowed our knees in the Greek Room. It was a help to us. Then I went to the History Room. After I had bowed my knees there just in front of the seat where I sat, nearly thirty years ago, I left, only to be met outside by John Mackenzie of Kiltearn. I asked him back into the room, where we had another praying session. On my knees then I was reminded of the fact that we had seven men in that classroom in my time — all professing the one faith, and of the same Church. Today only Murdo K. Murray and myself are left in the Free Church of that company. Dear Gregor Macleod lost his life on the high seas in the path of duty.* It was a day in which I was conscious of His love and care."

The last of these visits to which he refers was made as late as February 1981 while he was attending meetings of the Lord's Day Observance Society in Edinburgh. "To begin with," he recalls, "I made a visit to the College where I met for the first time the caretaker there.† It was very touching indeed to have a cup of tea from him and to sit in the old dining room while drinking it. Indeed, I sat in the place which I used to occupy at meals in my student days. How nostalgic all this was to me! The Lord reminded me of many things in that setting; most of all the godly people I then knew who are now in the great eternity. It moved me much that so many of my fellow-students are there also."

---

* Rev. Gregor Macleod and his wife, Elizabeth MacDonald, were lost at sea by enemy action while proceeding to the Free Church Mission field in South Africa.

† Mr William Anderson, who had been recently appointed.

While in College, James associated himself principally with the Elder Memorial Free Church, Leith, partly for reasons of territorial convenience, but principally because a highly-respected fellow-isles-man, Rev. John Shaw M.A., was minister there. Mr Shaw was a native of Harris, a man of genial disposition, and a diligent and judicious pastor.

There was a considerable Highland population in Edinburgh in those days, and each of the four major Presbyterian denominations had its own Gaelic charge. In addition, the Elder Memorial Church had a short Gaelic meeting after the Sabbath evening service, and James gave willing assistance with its maintenance. The Gaelic community of Edinburgh became warmly attached to him, and many hospitable homes were open to him and his like-minded companions. It was during this period that he made, or deepened, acquaintance with the ministers who became his chosen guides and counsellors in his ministry in North Uist — men like Kenneth A. MacRae, of Stornoway; Murdoch MacRae of Kinloch; Angus Finlayson of North Tolsta, and several others whose names come prominently into the reminiscences recorded in his diary.

\*     \*     \*     \*

It was as a student-preacher that Mr Morrison first faced a North Uist congregation. Forty years later, he recalls the event. "I arrived there on the 15th December 1936."

That visit had life-long consequences. North Uist wanted him back, and he came.

# CHAPTER THREE

# THE MINISTER OF THE WORD

**The chariot of God's providence runneth not upon broken wheels.**
—SAMUEL RUTHERFORD.

On 12th February 1977 Mr Morrison wrote in his diary, "My first period of service in North Uist as a preacher of the Gospel was in 1936. . . . That is now past the 40th milestone."

The North Uist that he came to know then was, in respect of social amenities at least, much less attractive than it is today, and had little to offer a prospective pastor. In terms of accessibility the island was indeed remote. There were no planes offering swift and comfortable transportation from Glasgow to Benbecula; such an idea could find its place only in a pipe-dream! From the rather bleak ports of Kyle of Lochalsh and Mallaig, sturdy but slow steamships braved the storms of the West to deposit their passengers and goods on Lochmaddy pier at whatever times wind and weather might allow. They might not reach at the scheduled times, but the point was, *they got there eventually!* David MacBrayne and Sons were the principal carriers, and their record for safe transportation was good. Their virtual monopoly of the coastal trade was the theme of an irreverent parody of a Psalm.

> The earth belongs unto the Lord
> And all that it contains,
> *Except Argyll and the Western Isles,*
> *And that is all MacBrayne's.*

But to poke fun at MacBrayne's was the exclusive right of the people principally served, certainly not of outsiders and casuals! Sir Archibald Geikie, in his *Scottish Reminiscences,* tells of an English clergyman who, while awaiting, on Tobermory pier, the steamboat that was to take him to

Skye, accosted a Highlander who was leaning against a wall, smoking his pipe. When, he asked, was the boat for Skye expected?

"Out came the pipe, followed by the laconic answer, 'That's her smoke', and the speaker pointed in the direction of the Sound of Mull. . . . When at last the steamer itself rounded the point and came fully into sight, it seemed to the clergyman a much smaller vessel than he had supposed it would be, and he remarked to the Highlander 'That the Skye steamer! that boat will surely never get to Skye'. The pipe was whisked out again to make way for the indignant reply, 'She'll be in Skye this afternoon, *if nothin' happens to Skye'.*"

— 1 —

An added inconvenience for the inhabitants of the Uist group of islands was that the means of transportation between these islands themselves tended to be infrequent and irregular; there were few scheduled ferries. It took the pressures of national defence to produce the good roads and inter-linking causeway that have brought such improved conditions of travel and communication to the islands concerned. A competent knowledge of navigation and general seamanship would therefore be a distinct advantage for a man taking a pastoral oversight of any of these islands in those earlier times. That was one of the many qualifications that James Morrison had when, in 1942, as a licentiate of the Church, he accepted a call to North Uist. An islesman himself, he understood the people, their way of life, their outlook and interests. He spoke their language and cherished their culture with an enthusiasm that some would regard as bordering on fanaticism. The Gaelic language was to him what Hebrew was to the Jew; indeed, he himself often made that comparison. He held that where Gaelic went out as a spoken language Gaeldom lost more than just a language; it lost an ethos, a way of life, that was quite inseparable from the language. The remnant of the Celtic heritage that remained was little more than the grin on the face of the Cheshire cat, in *Alice in Wonderland,* that

17

lingered on for a little, after the cat itself had disappeared. You just could not retain the grin for long after the cat had gone; and the Gaelic ethos could not long survive the disappearance of the language.

It was this conviction that made him so resistant to the encroachment of an alien culture. To keep Gaelic alive required more than an annual Comunn Gaidhealach Mod. It must be spoken in the home. It must be taught in the school. It must be the language of the people in their public worship. If there were visitors present in Church who did not know Gaelic, by all means let "a word in English" be added for their benefit. But the conducting of the whole service in English was not to be expected! Even the Presbytery came under his reproof when, in his absence on one occasion, it lapsed into conducting its opening worship in English! He recalls: "On arriving I said to the moderator there and then that the worship must be what it had always been, in Gaelic. And it was; even the prayer in constituting the Presbytery was in Gaelic. Nothing was allowed to hurt the finest and best, indeed the business was geared to further the very opposite of that."

So, for the time being at least, the situation was saved.

— 2 —

When, in 1943, Mr Morrison married Nurse Annie Macleod, of Melbost, Lewis, he brought to the Free Church Manse of North Uist a true help-meet. Calm, controlled prudent and unfailingly courteous, she was the perfect counterpart to her more impetuous husband. And he knew it! And said it! And saw the hand of God in it all! He writes in this connection: "How thoughtful God was when He prepared a wife for me who could enter into all my experiences and duties with heartfelt love and adoration! Today, we were on holiday again; and we exercised ourselves accordingly. I wouldn't say that my good lady handles or conceives of money as I do. At the same time she handles it more wisely than I do. Mr Macrae, Stornoway, once referred to money as a sacred thing. Well, I should like to reckon it so too, but sacred in order to *spend* it well; not to *spare* it well!''

Mrs Morrison's spiritual background was very similar to that of her husband, and she shared with him a constant sense of indebtedness to the teaching and example of godly parents. A diary entry dated 1st September 1972 records a visit to her old home on that day. ''After lunch we made our way to Melbost. My dear wife and her sister, Jessie, had their hearts full as they walked over their father's croft and the haunts of their youth, including the road they traversed on their way to school. This same human and natural element must have gripped the heart of Joseph, when he saw his brethren and heard the language of his boyhood on their lips. Well, these are emotions that can mean much in their own right, but they are particularly intense when to nature, even in its most compelling mood, are added holy and sweet memories of worthy parents as they gathered their children round the family altar night and day and from one end of the year to the other, to praise and magnify the name of God together. Reflections such as these accompanied us as we moved quietly along these familiar paths and meadows. I have always personally benefited by a visit to this lovely spot of His creation.''

The marriage-bond between this choice couple was never strained. It was ''in the Lord'', and they were careful to maintain it in that character. They began and ended each day on their knees together before God, seeking His blessing upon their home and congregation, with sympathetic mention of those in special need. They committed large portions of Scripture to memory — including the whole of Psalm 119! They read their daily portions systematically, with James interjecting comments on the verses read, so as to bring out their meaning more clearly. They often went visiting together, especially when the minister was on his pastoral rounds. And when Mrs Morrison, occasionally, was absent from home for a day or two, the minister and his dog, Jet, were partners in disconsolation. Writing on one of these occasions, the lonely husband says, ''I love her more than ever. I was glad to have Jet with me; I am positive he misses her. I have never heard before the type of whine he has — with two or three grace notes in it all.''

Because of their full understanding of each other, they could discuss matters in which they differed with complete frankness and without the fear of evoking resentment. If James at any time went beyond the accepted bounds of prudence and tolerance in his public relations, his wise and cautious wife would be the first to tell him so and, on reflection, he would agree with her judgment, for, to him, her very admonition was a benediction.

On the occasions they were not able to kneel together in household prayer they remembered each other in their private devotions and were strengthened and comforted. Regarding one of his many absences from home James writes: ''I was moved at worship as I recollected His over-shadowing of me throughout the Communion season at Staffin. It wasn't the consciousness of comfort that I enjoyed in the services that touched me most. It was the fear of the Lord that rested on my spirit, preserving me in all the ways of the Lord and constraining me to deliver His message to men. My wife and I had mutual benefit from our sharing of one another's experiences since I had left her the week before. We both could testify of being much in prayer for one another.''

Their last family worship together in 1978 became the subject of the following comment: ''Worship had a very solemn emphasis for us; it was a further reminder that here we have no continuing city. My very dear wife said at this time last year: 'Who knows if we both should see the end of another year?' Well, here we are at the end of 1978 and we are in good health and in love with one another more than ever; and the best of all in Christ Jesus — to live and die with Him; for to be with Christ is *far better;* that is our conscious assurance also.''

He expands his thought in a later entry. ''One of the ingredients in my longing for heaven is the prospect of praising His name forever. That itself makes me pant — at least at times — for heaven as a place where I shall be able to exalt God, as against my slowness of heart to exercise myself thus here. If I were altogether innocent without any personal experience of such an evil heart of unbelief I could and would not believe that any human heart could fall from such a height of innocence to such a depth of degradation and unbelief.''

— 3 —

Rumour has it that preachers are bad listeners, and rumour sometimes has truth on her side. But, contrary perhaps to the general impression of him, Mr Morrison could not be included among the defaulters. His diary jottings show that he listened carefully and critically, but not captiously. Thin doctrine, indeed, failed to stir his palate, especially if there was evidence of scrappy preparation. One un-named offender, in this respect, is dismissed with the comment that he ''used the inelegancy of his Gaelic as an excuse for the poverty of his thought''. A lay-speaker at a Gaelic fellowship-meeting, whose verbosity was becoming intolerable, was interrupted with the remark, ''That will do for the present: you may sit down.'' But such strictures were rare, and his references to speakers — especially to his helpers at his Communion services — were usually generous even to a fault.

Slipshod reading of the Scriptures and faulty accentuation of the Gaelic language he could not away with. The Lord's message deserved our best — even to the last detail. Precentors sometimes came under his reproof for their muffled articulation of the line at the Gaelic services. Such a rendering completely nullified the purpose of the exercise.

But the severest criticisms in the diary are directed against himself. Take, for instance, this entry which refers to a recorded reproduction of one of his own sermons, and the line of reflection to which it gave rise. ''I listened to a word on a tape, which I delivered in Grimsay about a year ago. It was a good word but it left me somewhat frightened, for it was too objective altogether. I need to enter the field of conflict more; I need to live in the hearts of His own more. I am full of confusion. And it is so enervating to labour on without seeing fruit for one's labours. I have also become conscious of a strong dislike of visitation; indeed to remain indoors without making any personal contacts at all would suit my mood of late through and through.''

And again: ''Continued my studies in Luke 11: 13, 14 — The heavenly host, and the heavenly song. The word 'host' denotes (a) Multitude; (b) Order — military precision here; (c) Unity; (d) Service. (2) The themes of the song (a) Glory, Peace to God and Goodwill, (b) The highest it brings heaven and earth together; (c) God and men. I had prayer again and again but I felt that climate was against me. Prayer in Church was tense and superficial. But service on the whole was good.''

— 4 —

Mr Morrison's diary abounds in appreciative comments on sermons which he had heard from visitors to his own pulpit and from preachers to whom he had listened in other churches and in religious gatherings throughout the country. Almost invariably, his praise is lavish. The humblest effort won his commendation if he thought it represented the preacher's best and was directed solely to the glory of the Saviour and the salvation of the sinner. But woe betide the man who gave himself airs in the pulpit! Not that he spent many words on him; it was by studied economy of words rather than by unbridled volubility that he expressed himself in such cases. We have heard him quote Denney's dictum, in a gathering that included not a few preachers, that ''no man can at one and the same time create the impression that he himself is a great preacher, and that Jesus Christ is a great Saviour''. But where there was evidence of a zeal for Christ, no one in the audience responded more warmly than James Morrison.

Once, while on a visit to Glasgow, he saw two young people holding what turned out to be an open-air religious meeting. This was how he reacted to it. ''What a pleasant surprise I had in the afternoon! Walking down Sauchiehall Street in the afternoon I witnessed a fair crowd and the attraction was a young woman giving her testimony; this was followed by an address from a young man on 'violence'.

22

The new Church was opened on 20th June 1950 — the day before the induction of the Rev. Malcolm Morrison to Scalpay. The dedication prayer was offered by Rev. James Morrison.

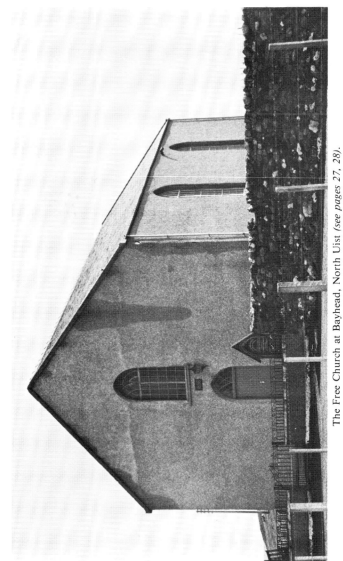

The Free Church at Bayhead, North Uist (*see pages 27, 28*).

I couldn't help admiring them, and after a bit I was quite ready to step forward myself. I, however, refrained from doing so, for I was anxious to let the young folk have their say."

The writer of those lines was surely of the affinity of Bunyan's Mr Standfast who testified to those who assembled to witness his departure: "I have loved to hear my Lord spoken of; and wherever I have seen the print of His shoe in the earth, there have I coveted to set my foot too."

James Morrison saw "the print of His shoe" in Sauchiehall Street that day, and his heart went out to the young people who had drawn his attention to it.

C

# CHAPTER FOUR

# RE-BUILDING THE WALLS

*Much more profitable and gracious is doctrine by example than by rule.*
—SPENCER.

When James Morrison became minister of the Free Church in North Uist he came to a community which urgently needed a man of his initiative. There had indeed been a succession of godly and able ministers in the pastorate, but the ministries for the most part had been short, and the vacancies in between had been of long duration, with the result that, church-wise, the morale of the people had deteriorated. For lack of strong leadership the church buildings had gone into disrepair. The affairs of God's house had become secondary. Added to this, the people, for the most part, had little more than what allowed for a bare existence. It was a daunting situation for a young man to face, but James took up the challenge with a courage that gradually rallied the dispirited congregation around him. Although money was hard to come by, he saw that resources in voluntary labour were not lacking. His appeals for help had the enforcement of personal example. A stocky, strongly-build man, it was not in him to call for help from others while he himself stood aside merely exercising an oversight of the work. In the emergency, he discovered that he had skills that could be developed in the Church's interests. He could repair pot-holed paths and roadways! With skilled advice, he could mix and apply concrete and plaster! He could saw wood to prescribed lengths and wield a hammer constructively! He was not afraid of heights and could sit confidently in a bosun's chair! Helpers gathered around him and the work of restoration proceeded with a momentum commensurate with the material resources available. It was a long and testing struggle, but there was no relaxation. There were, of course, the usual critics — the Sanballats and Tobiases, as James calls them in his diary where he reviews the events of those days — men whose only contribution to the work was to criticise, to deride and to hinder; but the work continued. While the Manse still remained scarcely habitable, the church was brought back into reasonable comfort; the sturdy islanders were not looking for luxury.

— 1 —

One day, during this period, James was on the train, bound for Glasgow in the interests of the work, when a fellow-passenger in the compartment, a self-confessed Communist, began to proclaim his political faith. A minister, of course, was an obvious target. Ministers were parasites on society, alleged the Marxist. They lived on others. They did not know what real work was. They had never done a hard day's work in their lives!

James had had enough. Opening his hands, palms uppermost, he exclaimed, "Friend, our hands will show what experience we have of manual labour. There are mine; now let us see yours." The challenge was repeated, supported by the other passengers, and reluctantly accepted. The hands of the minister showed signs of toil more convincingly than did the hands of his critic! The hands which the Carpenter of Nazareth laid in blessing upon the children of Galilee bore the marks of manual toil; and so to the end, did the hands which James Morrison raised in benediction over the people of North Uist whom the Lord had laid upon his charge.

"Nothing succeeds like success," says Dumas, and the truth of the adage was amply demonstrated by this work of restoration at Bayhead, where the central church is situated. Having succeeded in one place the congregation were more easily persuaded to turn their attention to another. The buildings in Sollas were repaired, and in the island of Grimsay, a new church and Mission-house were erected. Mr Morrison's money-raising efforts were unconventional but effective. He would call a congregational meeting and set the whole project before them, and then appeal to the people individually to indicate the measure of financial support that might be expected from them. The method did not quite accord with the Master's counsel, "Let not thy left hand know what thy right hand doeth", but Jesus was rebuking the ostentatious giving of the Pharisees, whereas James Morrison was appealing to the faith and generosity of the good people of North Uist. And the pledges which they gave were duly honoured, and in many cases, exceeded.

— 2 —

Mr Morrison had begun this work in faith and with much prayer, and it rejoiced his heart to see the hand of God in the sustained support of his people. Again and again he pours out his gratitude in his diary entries. One gift that touched him deeply became the subject of articles in the local press. An entry dated 2nd April 1979 runs: "My first duty was the preparation of a somewhat lengthy and important article for the *Stornoway Gazette* and the *Oban Times*. It was a description of a Gothic Arch window of teak material, and with coloured glass, which was made for us free of charge by a young man from the congregation who is a college lecturer in building, carpentry and joinery at Clydebank Technical College. One of our senior ministers who inspected the window reckoned that it would have cost us around £1,000 as at present set in the Church here." And James invokes God's blessing upon the donor.

Lobster-fishing and processing had now been developed in Uist and Grimsay, and the fishermen were acknowledging God's providence in their increased prosperity by giving to His cause in accordance with the golden rule of "as God had prospered" them.

— 3 —

Throughout the remainder of Mr Morrison's ministry this interest in the maintenance of the Church's building continued. Progress was slow, for the work was extensive, and the costs kept mounting. Not until July 1978 was the last section of the roof completed in the Bayhead Church. It was an anxious time for the minister and his helpers. The summer Communion services had been arranged for the end of the month as usual, in the full expectation that the church would be ready for the occasion. But the rain descended and the floods came, and frustrated workers had to be transferred to other work where the state of the weather did not matter so much. By the time the storm abated it seemed impossible that the outstanding work could be completed in time. Came Saturday, 22nd July, with just three working days left before the Communion services were due to begin, and there the minister's diary takes up the story. "At worship," he writes, "I sought to plead for His compassion but He seemed just to wave me off altogether; in any case, no work was attended to all day — except what I did myself. It was a painful day for me in the region of the spirit. . . . In prayer I poured out my complaints before His throne, and He eased my smart. I wait on God, and my hope is in His Word. I trust that by Wednesday night I will have unbelief under my knees."

But the unfavourable weather continued, and faith was sorely tried. The story continues on Monday, 24th July.

"With the weather so challenging, all seemed to be against us. We prayed and prayed but the rain continued. God did not fail us however, for the slater appeared, and he did quite a fair amount of work. Further, we have the promise of three joiners for tomorrow. My own dear one is confident that our God will see to it that all shall be ready. As I write this, the weather is very threatening. The Lord sits on the flood and He is ever King."

Actually, *four* joiners turned up the next day, but there was still much left to try Mr Morrison's faith. "The Church was in such a mess inside, and the roof was a worry to me. Yes, but there was a calm underneath it all that I could not account for."

By 3.15 p.m. on the Wednesday, the joiners were finished, and the mopping up began. "A large contingent of women" arrived, and by the time they were finished late that night, the transformation was complete. Faith had been rewarded; God had kept His Word. The minister's record of that day is eloquent of gratitude. "When we visited the Church last night" he writes, "it was obvious that the Lord was in our midst and for us. It was spotlessly clean and the work done was illustrative of His covenant care. Blessed ever be His Name!"

— 4 —

Mr Morrison's joy during the Communion season that followed was derived not only from the presence and preaching of the two friends who assisted him, but from a faith that had triumphed over trial. On Monday evening, reflecting on the Communion, he wrote, "Attendance was the best for many years. Worship had the same fragrance for us in the morning and again in the evening. He changes not. Just as a coin that is dropped is found in the very place that claimed it; so we find the Lord has not changed when by fasting and prayer we return to the very place where we had lost faith in Him. This was another fine day; the weather has been very kind all the way. How indebted to the Lord we should be for His great mindfulness of us! The Welsh slate looks well on the Church and the work is without compare. Indeed there is not another roof like it in the whole Island; the appearance is superb; the quality of the work is superb; the finish is superb. God has done this through and through, and He used us all in our different capacities to effect it. I trust that this outflowing of His long-suffering and tender mercies may lead us to repentance. The Lord speak, and speak again, in accents loud and clear, for the salvation of sinners in all this."

The re-roofing of the Bayhead Church was the last major work of restoration carried out by Mr Morrison, and when the home-call came to him less than two years later he left with his congregation a group of buildings where they could worship in comfort, and a Manse and Mission-house where the ministers and missionaries of coming days could enjoy a fair measure of the amenities of modern life.

It was characteristic of the man that he left his own household comforts to the last, and was content with little, with the result that the Manse became the first call on the

28

resources of the congregation after his death. But they had learned much regarding Christian stewardship under his guidance and, in loyalty to his memory, they faced the work with courage and confidence.

# CHAPTER FIVE

# THE MAN OF AFFAIRS

*I have no faith in the altruism that makes the last war
the standard of the life of the community.*

—SAMUEL CHADWICK.

It may well be that Mr Morrison's organising ability was
first proved to himself and to the people around him by the
early success of his efforts in structural restoration. He
acquired a reputation for getting things done, and it was
evident that his interest in the well-being of the wider
community was a personal and constant concern to him. At
all events, when he was urged to place his talents at the
service of the District Council, and, later, the County
Council, he came to see that such service would be fully
consonant with his work as a minister of the Gospel, and
would give him a platform from which to proclaim man's
duty to man as the obvious corollary of man's duty to God.
The faith that he preached concerned all the interests of
man, temporal and spiritual. It related to society in general;
to social and industrial relationships, as well as to the fundamental problem of man's relation to God.

— 1 —

His work as a County Councillor necessitated frequent
visits to Inverness, the normal meeting-place of the Council,
and it brought him into contact with people whose outlook
was often very different from his own, and whose sense of
values, in some cases, was entirely materialistic. To these,
the new Councillor from North Uist was just an insular
eccentric, a religious enthusiast whose views might carry
some weight among his own people and in the local District·
Council, but certainly not in the wider forum of the County
Council. Some tried to patronise him, but they soon

discovered that he had a mind of his own and would be no man's lackey. Dr James Begg was once described as "the champion of lost causes", and it must have seemed to some of James Morrison's contemporaries that he had inherited the title. But he knew that causes related to the kingdom of God are never lost, and he held to them with a tenacity born of strong confidence. Not infrequently, he used "great plainness of speech", but without meaning to be discourteous. "In my County Council work," he writes, "I am always conscious of the danger of being discourteous, disorderly, arrogant and proud in the presentation of my matter. Even on the human level I am anxious to be a man in every sense and in the best sense of the term. And, above all, I always want to be a prince of the household of faith. And God was my strength and shield today."

For the recommendations that came from the Highlands and Islands Development Board regarding the educational policy for the County he had nothing but scorn, and suggested that it might be known as "Operation Cuttle-fish", because he suspected a hidden Roman Catholic influence in it. Nor did he approve the Owner-Occupancy policy that was being advocated by the Crofters' Commission. "It should be called the Crofters' *Demission,*" he caustically remarks. A paragraph on the subject, which he wrote for discussion by his Presbytery reveals his anxiety for the future of crofting.

"For the last twelve years there has been such marked deterioration in both the quality and quantity of crofting in the Islands as has never been seen or witnessed since the beginning of time. It is a shocking state of affairs seeing lorry loads of potatoes being shipped across the Minch from the Black Isle and other areas, the same applies to bread, to milk, vegetables and other commodities. Even the supplying of all School Canteens in the Islands, with all such requirements by local labour would add its own quota of economic help at a time when every agency and authority is castigated for our unemployment figures."

His views on the "crofter-owner" proposal are more fully elucidated in a press-report dated 10th April 1967. It runs:

"Uist's fighting minister, Rev. James Morrison, Bayhead, last week spoke against the Crofters' Commission's proposals for legislation which will make crofters owners of their crofts. The suggestion, which has been widely acclaimed by crofters themselves is currently being studied by Scots Secretary Mr William Ross.

Mr Morrison, chairman of the island's district council and one of the most influential voices on Uist, feels that while the idea is well intended, it may have consequences which will not be in the long-term interests of crofters.

He fears particularly that given ownership of their own crofts, islanders may be induced to climb on the 'tourist band-wagon' and utilise most of their land to provide holiday accommodation.

Mr Morrison spoke of the vast tracts of land in Lewis lying uncultivated and derelict and said he hoped the Uist landscape would never become desecrated by chalets and caravans.

'I am not against ancillary industry,' he said, 'but this is something which will be entirely alien to the way of life in the islands.'

By letting holiday accommodation crofters could sit at home and earn money without lifting a finger.

'It could be the death knell of crofting on these islands and if crofting dies so will Uist,' warned Mr Morrison.

He sympathised with those crofters who were anxious to get dry cash simply to build up their homes and crofts but he was concerned that all too many would be willing to let their crofts decline for the short-term rewards of tourism.

Crofting, he said, was basic to the well-being of Uist and if it were to be abandoned then the authorities might as well evacuate the islands.

The present system of crofting tenure which gave the landlord and the Land Court certain rights and worked well and ought not to be changed without very careful consideration.

Mr Morrison added that he was currently collecting evidence on what the effects of the new proposals might be.

Mr Morrison pointed out that many crofters were already

selling land for the rocket range extension in South Uist and while they might be regarded as 'fringe crofters', what was happening was bound to affect the crofter who was devoted to the land. Crofting needed townships and manpower to remain alive and the rocket range threatened both.

In South Uist, where they had already tasted cash, the crofters were all the more ready to 'sell their birthright for a mess of pottage', he said.''

An entry dated 20th January 1969, again underlines his anxiety for the future of crofting: ''Discussed with Donald Macdonald, Tarbert, the latest pipedream of the Crofters' Commission, for the crofters. I was glad to note that he was awake to this new threat to the way of life of our beloved Islands. Every facility must be granted to certain irresponsible sections of our present day society! When they get their crofts into their hands they will soon hand them over to the best buyer and the Crofters' Commission will see to it that the buyer will be the man or woman who will sponsor tourism — caravans, chalets, etc. And the major and overruling consequence of all this will be the desecration of the Lord's Day and all that that represents.''

— 2 —

One of the ancillary industries which he welcomed and supported was the lobster processing factory which had been set up in Grimsay. He watched over its development with care. When trouble arose between the fishermen and the manager, Mr Morrison registered his anxiety in the following entry: ''Mr Hilleary, one of the Directors of the lobster factory, arrived at 10.00 a.m. We had heart to heart talks about the conditions of things in Grimsay. God grant that nothing should hinder or hurt this industry. It was a profitable discussion all the way. I impressed upon him the solemn claims of the Lord's Day in any future development that might emerge.''

The ''solemn claims of the Lord's Day'' were always present to his mind in these plans for Highland industry. He knew only too well that in a materialistic age very little respect would be paid to the time-honoured way of life in

33

the Highlands of Scotland when it stood in the way of industries that contemplated nothing but secular gain. He had seen how the secular interest had come uppermost in many parts of Scotland, and particularly in the Isle of Skye after the introduction of the Sunday ferries; and when he expressed the fear that Skye "could become a hippy island" he was not being an alarmist. Such things had already happened in some parts of the north where settlers of an undesirable kind had taken up quarters. Gladly would he share the amenities of the community with the right type of visitor, but he prized the spiritual heritage of the Highlands too dearly to barter it away for the mess of pottage which was being offered in its place.

The diary bounds in vignettes of the officials and more prominent members of the County Council with whom he discussed matters relating to their work, and although he was far removed from the general outlook of some of these men, he was generous in praise where he thought praise was due. His impressions of a meeting with the Highlands and Islands Development Board are recorded in an entry dated 10th October 1968: "We met the H.I.D.B. at 2.30 p.m. It was a good meeting. Professor Grieve gave a good account of himself. Lord Lovat spoke very wisely and well. I sincerely liked his emphasis on Agriculture and Fishing. I put in a word against the increase in freights and fares. It was 4.50 p.m. before we finished. Lord MacDonald came to me and said: 'That was a good speech you made'. I stressed the seriousness of this issue, that the older generation had their roots too deep in the islands to suffer transplantation now, but I went on to add that the rising generation would not tolerate these inequalities for long. What then! Just a repetition of St Kilda mass evacuation with no return."

For Lord MacDonald, as also for Sir Francis Walker, the Convener of the Council, Mr Morrison had the warmest regard, and the kindness that these public-spirited men always showed him revealed that this cordial esteem was fully reciprocated.

In Earl Granville, a nobleman with landed interests in North Uist, he had also the most happy relations. Both men had the welfare of the islanders at heart and had frequent discussions along these lines.

In times when the economic plight of the Highlands and Islands generally left so much to be desired it was imperative that every scheme for betterment should be welcomed and hopefully examined. To Mr Morrison, many of these were little better than gimmicks — the nostrums of starry-eyed visionaries who were, however, blind to the distant view. The prime need of the whole area, in his view, was the re-habilitation of the natural industries. Tourism and the setting up of rocket ranges and other military establishments were mere accessories that might well prove more costly than they were worth.

In this connection, Mr Morrison refers to a public meeting that was held in North Uist: "8th August 1969: At 6.30 p.m. an official from St Andrews House and Brigadier Winfield, who is in charge of the Rocket Range appeared at the Manse. We discussed the form of the meeting. Mr Hughes, the above official, was anxious that I should not oppose any of their proposals. My reply to that, however, was that I recognised the fishing industry as part of the warp and woof of life in our communities. The meeting in the School was well attended. I was the first to speak after the Defence Officials. I had the greatest ovation of all from the audience. The South Uist man did his best to encourage the Rocket Range; but 'greater is He that is in us that he that is in the world'. That is a word that has often encouraged me."

"This morning," he resumes, "we asked at worship to be led of the Lord in our meeting with the Secretary of State for Scotland. He and his associates — six of them — arrived here at 10 a.m. and they had tea with us. It was 11 a.m. before they left. I had met Mr Ross before. He is very human. After we discussed the proposed Rocket Range in its application to the fishermen he turned to me and said: 'You have made a good case for the fishermen, but why do I see potatoes being shipped to Lochmaddy? Why bring vegetables from the mainland; why bring bread, etc. across that Minch?' These were sensible questions; and the answer is, sheer laziness and bad leadership.''

Though not a Socialist himself, Mr Morrison found many qualities in Mr William Ross (later Lord Ross of Kilmarnock) which won his admiration. Of another meeting with him he writes: ''I was deeply concerned about the tremendous responsibilities of this whole day. It was arranged that we should meet the Secretary of State and his staff in Benbecula, that is members of North Uist, South Uist and Barra District Councils. After that, I, as Chairman of our District Council, was asked to have dinner with him in Stornoway at 8.00 o'clock that night. Our meeting in Benbecula was good, and I am hopeful of much good following it. On arriving at the Hotel in Stornoway the now customary introduction was in operation. I was glad, however, to note that the Secretary of State had a glass of orange juice in his hand and he was at once happy to hand me a glass of the same drink. I took a great liking to him and to one or two of his colleagues. But some of the locals simply disgusted me, for many of them left the impression with me that the cursed 'glass' was more important to them than anything else in the world.''

— 4 —

Mr Morrison's opposition to strong drink was of long standing. An experience that he had in Inverness during his County Council days reminded him of an incident of his childhood. He tells us about it: ''Last night I couldn't help seeing from my bedroom window the many young men and women — some of them I felt sure barely twenty — who emerged from a pit, a pub across the road, with evident signs of their being under the influence of drink. This pained me beyond words. The earliest recollection I have in life, when about three years of age is of my wandering on a street in Glasgow (where I was born) and being taken in hand by a publican with a white apron. That apron, and the individual himself, are still clear to me. I had slipped my parents and found my way there; that however, was the only anxious moment they ever had over me — at least, with regard to a pub, for I was never inside one again. I have never handled a glass of beer and the little taste I had of whisky, some thirty years ago, wouldn't harm a kitten. I feel consciously indebted to God for that protection, and for the fact that I have never in any way contributed one single copper to the drink traffic. I see the Cross of the Lord Jesus Christ in all this."

He was always greatly concerned about the increasing pressure of temptation to which the young people were being subjected. In this connection he writes: "After the Education Committee, I spoke to the Director about the Educational Institute of Scotland oracle in relation to the Licensing Laws prepared for Scotland. It was a shocking proposal they made that young children should be allowed to drink in a public bar, provided their parents were there with them, and that was considered 'Civilised Drinking'. The Director was shocked too, and he felt sure that this would soon be overturned by an official decision of the Educational Institute of Scotland. God in His compassion grant it!"

He makes a note of a casual contact with a tippler in one of his journeys on County business. A friend was with him: "We had a quiet time until 4.00 p.m. when we had coffee together. On our being seated at the table a visitor from Australia with a smell of drink about him, accosted me. He impressed me as a man who had a bit of Bible training, behind him. I left a word with him. He did not object to my being personal in this matter, but took refuge in the remark 'It is different in Australia'. I pointed out to him that if both of us dropped down from the roof of that building the law of gravity would see to it that death would take charge of both of us, whether we were British or Australian. He saw my point but he wanted a cover-up for himself at all costs. I felt thankful that I had an opportunity to speak to him, and to warn and woo him in the name of the Lord.

"C. H. Lewis says in his book: *Mere Christianity,* p. 70: God 'wants us to be simple, single-minded, affectionate and teachable, as good children are; but He also wants every bit of intelligence we have to be alert at its job, and in first-class fighting trim'. The man who is fond of his glass is at once disqualified in this area of operations in the name of the Lord. His shield was again my preservation and comfort all night."

— 5 —

The transference of the functions of the County Councils to District Councils was strongly disfavoured by Mr Morrison, principally because it would mean that, in the larger units, the administration would, in many cases, be taken over by people who were quite unfamiliar with the special problems of some areas, and who would not therefore have the special aptitude for handling them that might be expected from natives of these parts. He was particularly apprehensive regarding the effect that the new set-up would have on education, and it delighted him when a leading educationist in Inverness spoke critically in this connection, He writes: "7th July 1976: What a rebuke was administered lately by Inverness High School rector to the new regions; and his reference to the days of Inverness-shire in relation to Education was particularly pertinent. I relished it. Mr Anderson said: 'The state of Scottish education is like the peace of God in the respect that it passes all understanding, and the national situation is mirrored in the regional set-up. Like the Chinese we can give names to our year; this has been the year of the Paper Blizzard, the year of the cut-back of everything except regional administrative paper work. The key is regionalisation, which must be the biggest single national disaster since Flodden or Culloden. I sigh unashamedly for the days of Inverness-shire. There was then a human and personal touch. Now we have a remoteness reminiscent of a hiccup on Mars — and as meaningful. . . .'

The big little men in our Education Department will not relish this solid fare."

Somewhat later he writes in the same critical strain: "It has been rightly said that 'Education is preoccupied with making a living rather than with living a life'. Indeed this cult of mediocrity finds abundant expression in our day in many unnatural fads in dress and physical appearance; in a mad craze for mass amusements and sheer cowardly fear.''

The work of the Education Committee in the area of Religious Instruction comes in for sharp criticism. He writes (30th November 1977): ''Today at worship my soul was somewhat listless and I couldn't shake off this mood for most of the day. After a bit I sat down to a piece of solid writing. It was part of my analysis of papers sent to our local school for their guidance in the so-called Religious Instruction exercises. This package of Scottish Education Department pretensions and puerilities does indeed sadden and sicken anyone devoted to the Cause of Truth and Righteousness. The documents cover the Pagan Cults that are abroad in the world in a manner that suggests that they qualify for the same faith and respect as the Scriptures of Truth themselves. I endeavoured to point out the origin and end of this modern syncretism.''

A further reference to proposed changes in administration indicates the kind of change that he would welcome: ''Replied to letter from Magnusson of the *Scotsman,* and filled in questionnaire. Added as a 'remark': 'The present Highland Administration is the product of commonsense, of experience of the hard facts of life and the mature judgments resulting therefrom. I have little confidence in the originators and promoters of the changes now envisaged. And their ''itch'' for change in nearly every instance, has reference to what has proved worthwhile and workable in every generation. It is our present philosophy of life that needs changing. In the words of Truth: 'Israel has forgotten his Maker and buildeth temples'. What is called for is not a change of Administration but a change of heart. We need in plain words a love for our work revealing itself in honest and faithful service.'''

— 6 —

Sometimes, like Moses under provocation, James Morrison under similar pressure, ''spake unadvisedly with his lips'' to his own subsequent regret. In this connection the following excerpt is revealing. ''I had a sure token of God's

39

D

care in the Chairman's Committee in the late afternoon. Before I left my room in the hotel I lightly decided not to open my mouth at the meeting. Immediately I was reminded that my mouth was not my own. I fell on my knees and asked the Lord to help me to do my duty. And I sincerely felt, at the meeting, that He had answered my prayer.''

His influence in frustrating the schemes of men who were opposed to his way of thinking, predictably, gave rise to opposition when the next election came round. When he learned of this, the effect was the opposite of what might have been expected. He had really been thinking of retiring from this form of public service, but the challenge of his opponents was not to be ignored or misread. If they thought that they could overturn his work, or discredit him in the eyes of the electorate, let them try! His vindication, he felt sure, would come from God. So he yielded to the importunities of his former sponsors to stand again.

The result was more than he had hoped for. On the day after the poll, he writes: ''10th May 1973: 'I had a lovely sleep after all the excitement as the evening wore on. And what a cancellation it was of all the vain hopes of the radical party here! My opponent attracted only 68 votes, while I had 324. I trust I shall always prove worthy of this trust. I am persuaded that many of the young stood by me, too. The volume of acknowledgments I have received is quite impressive. One of my colleagues visited me to see if I would be willing to continue as Chairman of our Council. I indicated that I would. This has had its origin somewhere else, and I know what it means. God preserve to us the mind of the Lord in all our doings, unto the very end.''

— 7 —

When, finally, Mr Morrison decided that he should resign from the Council, he was greatly relieved that Rev. Roderick Macleod, the Church of Scotland minister of Berneray, was willing to stand for the vacancy. He writes: ''After I had spent a period in the garden Mr McLeod from Berneray called at 11 a.m. I signed his paper for a new landmark in his life. He hopes to qualify for the Western Isles Authority —

as a County Councillor. We had prayer together and we had a persuasion that the Lord was for us in it all. May it please God ever to prosper us in all our concerns. He was pleased to preserve and prosper me beyond all my expectations."

He returns to the subject later: "The prospective Councillor, Rev. R. MacLeod, Berneray, and I made a few calls — twenty-one in all — in the interests of the good cause. We were anxious to do our duty and, at every turn, we made our prayer to Him."

The eventual election of Dr Macleod gave Mr Morrison great satisfaction, and he regarded it as an answer to prayer. Like himself, Dr Macleod belonged to the Western Isles and had a competent knowledge of the needs of the whole area. A man of scholarly attainments, he had at heart the welfare of the people and would do his utmost to see that these were kept before the administrative bodies.

Mr Morrison reviewed his long experience of local government with gratification, although not with complacency. In December 1973 he writes: "I have in large measure become immune in public life to the fear of man. I have gained much valuable experience in local government affairs; I have seen quite a number of major improvements in both the secular and sacred areas of life in North Uist that the Lord has prospered through my instrumentality. I know, too, that the tempo of life in sound exegesis of the Word, in a more spiritual appreciation of the doctrines of grace, in a more consistent acknowledgment of God in providence, have prospered."

He adds, "My life since I quitted local government work has been more or less free of much confusion and strife". More than ever his time and energy were given to the work of Christ and His Church. But it probably would not be wrong to say that not until he was removed from them did the people of North Uist fully appreciate all that he had done for their welfare in all the departments of his activity. Some of the causes that he championed were not popular, and his successes in them were limited. But he was not discouraged. Paul's message to the Corinthians, he believed, was addressed to him also; *"be ye stedfast, unmoveable, always abounding in the work of the Lord, forasmuch as ye know that your labour is not in vain in the Lord.''*

So he transcribed into his diary a prayer which he had read in a magazine to which he subscribed: ''Our Father in Heaven, give us the long view of our work and our world. Help us to see that it is better to fail in a cause that will ultimately succeed than to succeed in a cause that will ultimately fail. . . . Through Jesus Christ our Lord. Amen.''

# CHAPTER SIX

# THE MAN OF PRAYER

**Prayer brings the Divine omnipotence into the occasions of life.**
— D. M. MacINTYRE.

It did not require a long association with James Morrison to discover that he was, in an unusually marked degree, a man of prayer. "I love to have a hunger," he once wrote, "something like a gnawing pain, for prayer." He distinguished between *going aside* to pray, and *being called* to prayer. It was the sense of being called aside by God that made the exercise so delightful. Prayer without urgency never satisfied him. "I had a good day at my studies," he records on one occasion, "at the same time I missed a pressure of prayer in it all."

His entry for 18th October 1967 contains the following paragraph: "Prayer as one of the special exercises of faith is rightly concerned with the application of Christ to the soul — Christ as the healing balm to the sick soul; Christ as the word to those who are guilty before God; Christ as our wisdom, righteousness, sanctification and redemption. Prayer is a tuning fork which gives the soul and life of a Christian its proper note and sets the pitch of all the sweet and heavenly music his life is capable of. Without prayer it is as impossible to regulate and attune the soul and life thus as it is to awaken a dead corpse to such a holy ministration. God grant me such an anointing, such a sure token of the love of the Spirit, of my interest in the Saviour's atonement, and the persuasion that I am loved of the Father. Prayer is never satisfied with appearances, half-truths, and superficialities in any avenue of the Christian life. Prayer — that is prayer in the Spirit — brings the soul into unison with the letter of Scripture and the spirit thereof; it enables the soul to die with Christ and suffer with Him; it also makes it gloriously possible for the soul to live and reign with Christ.''

Urgency in prayer, he held, required a continual sense of personal need and unworthiness: ''It is a pointer to the judgment that has overtaken us that prayers are heard without any reference to sin at all. I find this in our own limited communion here too. I often think of my worthy grandfather. Hearing him in prayer I would find fault with him that he would so often refer to his sin. When he touched a holy and sweet aspect of Truth I would be moved at once. I then would be so grieved that he should refer to sin any more. Today I think otherwise for I can see that any special inspiration granted to him he would employ at once to hit sin in his heart. In other words his life of faith was directed at the end of sin and the bringing in of an eternal righteousness. God so love me too!''

— 1 —

Intermittent supplication was not enough. The Christian must ''pray without ceasing''. ''The vision of God,'' says Bishop Westcott, ''makes life a continuous prayer.'' It covers everything. Dr John Kennedy tells us in his sketch of Alister Og, of Edderton, that ''on one occasion there came a pious man to consult with him about the meaning of the counsel, 'Pray without ceasing'. On his arrival he found Alister busy digging his croft. 'You are well employed, Alister,' he said on coming up to him. 'If delving and praying, and praying and delving, be good employment, I am' was his answer, which met the enquirer's difficulty before he had stated it.''

That was how James Morrison prayed. When he was preaching in places where church and manse might be some considerable distance apart he preferred to walk because, as he explains, this gave him a better opportunity, and more time, to be in fellowship with God on his way to the pulpit, and on his way home after having delivered his message. As he walked he prayed.

The custom was maintained also out of consideration of the physical benefit derived. Quoting G. M. Trevelyan, he writes, "I have two doctors, my left leg and my right". And they served him well, to the very end.

— 2 —

Visitors to the hospitable Manse at Bayhead during Mr Morrison's ministry are not likely to forget his intercessions at family worship. North Uist especially was covered; the very machairs and the moors where the cattle and sheep fed; the kyles and bays around the shores which the Lord had stocked with all manner of fish for the good of men; the fields producing their annual yield of food which betokened God's unfailing care for His creatures — all came in for mention. All the interests of the people were commended to the loving care of the Lord of all. Recalling the experiences of the day on 7th January 1977 he writes: "Again and again I was called to my knees. On one of these occasions I made my supplications on behalf of all the congregation. I began at Newton Ferry and covered all to Kallin, Grimsay."

"Nothing like prayer," he writes again, "to order one's affairs, whatever they be — whether of heaven or of earth." He submitted himself to God's guidance in his County Council work just as in the duties which fell to him in his labours as a minister of the Word. An entry regarding forthcoming meetings in Inverness reveals the spirit in which he approached his work. "So far," he writes, "I have clear proof of his hearing my prayer when, on Monday, I poured out my heart to Him, to cover me all week, to use me for good at all times. At today's meeting I spoke against the irresponsibility of lowering the safeguards that are left to protect our young from strong drink. I had a sweet fragrance in my room all day and all night and that holy unction that accompanies prayer. And blessed be His name He honoured me in calling me again and again to His feet to make my requests known to Him. After I came in from my meeting, I was happy to bow before His sovereignty, then after lunch I again set Him before me. On arriving back home at 6.10 p.m. I was constrained to do the same. And for the remainder of the night my soul was kept in constant peace before Him."

We have further glimpses of him at prayer in the following entries:

## At His Feet

"It was my desire today that I should learn from the Samaritan, who with a loud voice glorified God and fell on his face at the feet of Jesus giving Him thanks. What a holy and happy place, to be in, *at His feet*. I think I know a little of that experience. I know too that I desire more conformity to this pattern as I journey on."

## Self-Watch

"I was too much the prey of my emotions in preaching today with the result that my spirit was hardly in action properly at all. I must exercise continual watch over this constitutional weakness — emotion. It has a place and it can be used with great effect as a lubricant, but not as a control.

## The Lure of Mammon

"I was much in prayer that He would love our people this day in all their ways — the fishermen and the crofters having their special place in all this. I am anxious lest Satan should find an occasion against us. Over the years the fishermen, without one exception, laid aside their fishing for the whole Communion season. With such money going now the temptation is greater to change all this. Our God is the same and He is able to save us and them. Our hearts are set on this, that we should once again have a time of love on the Mount of ordinances."

## Night-Vigils

"W.S.W. Showery and fairly strong winds. *Anxious about children's crossing to Uig* for re-opening of Schools. Wakened a few times during night and was led to pray for them every time — for travelling and other mercies. But my highest concern is that they should all fear God and honour the Queen."

## Prayer and Praise

"I am very concerned about how I address God in prayer. I am also much in prayer for the congregational praise. I don't think of my *text* in this. I think more of all who are to hear *the Word;* that the praise should be representative of their needs; their responses to God and their acceptance in Him."

No area of activity was left uncovered. "When I endeavour to pray in the interest of the Gospel, I also remember my County Council work, the Church properties and my gardening concerns. May His blessing accompany and rest on all."

— 4 —

It was said of William Chalmers Burns that "his whole ministry was a series of battles fought at the mercy-seat". The same could be said of James Morrison — right to the end. For he was not far from the end when he wrote in review of the day: "My vain and earthly mind seemed to barricade itself against any worthwhile contact with God; it was determined to keep me from my knees at all costs. From the first part of the day this neutralisation of all my spiritual powers kept me at bay. However, once I found my knees I contacted the power; nothing could hold me after that. It reminded me of my boyhood when a few of us could hold a fishing boat with her engine going before she could move from the pier. As long as we held her stationary her propeller or propellers could not effect a single movement forward; if we allowed a little slackening of the pressure and the boat moved a little from us, nothing would avail any more to stop her."

Public service had its special trials and difficulties, but he faced them with prayer. "I have duties to face this coming week which are a source of concern to me," he writes; "God be at my right hand and let me not be moved. Lord save Uist!"

## Journeying Mercies

"It turned out a wild afternoon and I made this a matter of prayer in order that I should travel home in time and in

47

comfort and by the time I went aboard at Uig at 8 p.m. the whole scene had changed — the wind had nearly ceased. It was a fine run home and I had some relish in prayer during the journey, too. How I should praise God for the spirit of prayer! And on arriving home I found my dear wife well and happy to have me home once again. My soul should ever magnify God for His interest in me personally but I feel more indebted to Him for my being privileged to further His cause and work in the Church and in the world.''

### "Lord, teach us to pray"

"While on my knees I was led to pray in the words of 1 Tim. 1: 17: Now unto the king eternal, immortal, invisible, the only wise God, be honour and glory for ever and ever, Amen. As I poured out my soul in petition after petition I did so along the lines of this prayer. I desired to be under the impression of His Kingly reign and the eternity of His being, of the incorruptible nature of His person, of the invisible character of His glory, of the wisdom of His administration particularly as all this applied to the great eternity.''

### Crucifying the flesh

"My flesh was vile to me all morning. After I had poured out my heart to God in prayer my smart was somewhat eased. Since the end of 1969 and up to this morning I have had a very even realisation of His loveliness about my spirit. It was just like a cloud of sweet incense nearly all the time.''

### The Christian's Perfection

"After I started my work in earnest I decided I would endeavour to pray every hour of the evening and night and I was enabled to realise this at least in the letter of it. It made my studies a pleasure in any case. I worked on 1 Peter 5: 10, particularly in 'God Himself will make you perfect'. I received much help from Goodwin on this theme. I emphasised the place of suffering in the Christian's experience here. The perfection noted here is not to be acquired in an easy chair, dreaming about temptation. This is the fruit of many dislocations and falls in one's conflict with Satan and sin. How grievous all such experiences are but that is the way through much pain and tribulation to attain this end."

## Fellowship with God

"Arrived Inverness at 4.30 p.m. I stayed in my room all evening. *God seemed to want me all for Himself.*"

## Prayer Encouragement

"We had a lovely spirit at worship today. I considered myself like a bird hovering over its young as I endeavoured to pray for Uist. I sought the Lord to put far from us whatever was unworthy of the Truth; that is any bitter root wherewith the land would be defiled. And I endeavoured to prepare myself for the prayer meeting at night. I had 1 Thess. 5: 23. It was good without a doubt."

## Prayer and Intercession

"It has been said that the impulse to pray, within our hearts, is evidence that Christ is urging our claims in heaven. Well that is part of my pain of late, that I am not all satisfied with the type of impulse that is present with me."

## Lack of Prayer

"I have been conscious for some time of a lack of prayer — that is, of the spirit of prayer. Perhaps the reason for it is that I have not been at my studies of late as I should have been; that also may account for my many maulings at the hands of unbelief. It is not so much my loss of confidence in the area of my acceptance with God that I am conscious of. It is the easy access that vain things have to my heart and to my tongue; the lack of deep concern I have for the souls of my poor people and the infrequency of my visits to the Throne of Grace."

— 5 —

Answers to prayer sometimes came very unexpectedly, as in the following experience: "Worship was alive with sanctified commonsense today. We considered in some

49

detail parts of Acts 17 — as we went along in our day's reading. Left for Stornoway at 3 p.m. No bus appeared at that hour and no one seemed to care to give us a lift. But I said a few times: 'When it pleases God, His man will arrive; we shall have our lift'. At the Melbost junction a bus from town dropped a passenger and prepared to return. He took us aboard and finally let us off at the very door we desired. And he charged us nothing and added: 'I had much pleasure in doing this. I met you coming off the plane in Inverness some time ago. I was on my way to the Royal Infirmary. On the following Wednesday you visited me and prayed with me in the Infirmary.' That touched me and spoke to me. Our steps were ordered that day.''

## Matters for Prayer

''On the way to the last meetings at 7.30 and 8.30 p.m. I decided in my walk to pray all the way. And as I did I sought to classify reasons for repentance as well as faith. I reflected on my forgetfulness of God, especially as I reviewed things as I went along. I reflected on the many, many occasions from early manhood I was exposed to temptations of various kinds. How God again and again, indeed times without number, preserved me when He could so easily have had me disgraced! I endeavoured to praise His great name for all this.

The Lord was by me all day. I lost my desk keys. After a fruitless search I bowed my knees before God for this. After this I was directed to them! Then a cheque I had received for County Council expenses went missing. I prayed about this too, and was heard.''

But the principal things always came uppermost. He writes, on another occasion: ''In Grace at the table this petition possessed me: 'Lord make this Island a nursery for the Church — of trees of righteousness the planting of the Lord that He might be glorified'.''

## Pastoral Oversight

''We should make a yearly survey of our own individual charges. We should cover every area of life within the bounds of our congregations; we should interest ourselves in the social, the industrial, the educational, the moral, the spiritual life of our individual areas of service. There is no use in one or two doing this; every member of Presbytery should be interested in this.''

## Fellowship in Prayer

*"Friday,* 1st January: We, my wife and Angus the elder, finished 1970 and began 1971 on our knees in prayer. We went over to Angus at 11 p.m. and we began our worship at 11.30 p.m. We have done this over the years and God has acknowledged His own word in all this without a single doubt. After we wished each other a good New Year I added that we should begin the year loving one another and Angus agreed that this is how it should be. God cover us in this as in all else. Service today was good. Text: Deut. 12: (1) The Lord's covenant interest in the land (a) He cared for it; (b) His eyes were upon it. (2) The enduring nature of this care (a) *always;* (b) from the *beginning to the end.* He seemed to encourage us by this word. God grant that we may see evidence of this as the year proceeds.''

## Given to Prayer

"I had a breath of prayer, and it improved as the day proceeded. Yes, He encouraged self-denial and a positive commitment to the interests of Truth and righteousness. I began with Ephes. 3, v. 19, the word I had arranged, or I should have said, the word that had been arranged for me — for the noon service tomorrow. When I finished it, I sought the Lord to bless it all to all — to me personally, to the saints and then to sinners needing the salvation of the Lord. On my knees — indeed I always fall on my face to the ground at such times — I asked that this whole message might enter my very bloodstream, and become part of me in every avenue of my spirit, soul and body.''

"Prayer,'' says Thomas Adam, "is *Want Felt; Help Desired;* with *"Faith to Obtain.''*

By that definition, James Morrison really *prayed.*

# CHAPTER SEVEN

# THE GROWING CHRISTIAN

**Christianity is hard but gainful and happy. I contemn the difficulty when I respect the advantage.**
—BISHOP HALL.

When James Morrison, as a young man, made profession of his faith in Christ he was already a settled believer. The apostolic injunction, "Examine yourselves whether ye be in the faith", had come to him with force, and to the very end it covered his Christian life. He would have agreed that "for one look at self the believer ought to take seven looks at Christ"; but even the "one look" ought to be there in the exercise of faith. We have heard him signify his profound agreement with Dr John Duncan, the beloved *Rabbi* in this connection. "For myself," discloses the *Rabbi,* "I cannot always come to Christ direct, but I can always come by sin. Sin is the handle by which I get Christ. I take a verse in which God has put Christ and sin together. I cannot always put my finger upon Christ, and say 'Christ belongs to me'; but I can put my finger upon sin and say, 'Sin belongs to me'. I take that word, for instance, 'The Son of Man is come to save that which was lost'. Yes, lost, lost, lost, — I'm lost. I put my finger upon that word and say, 'I'm the lost one; I'm lost'. Well, I find that 'the Son of Man is come to save the lost'; and I cry out 'What God hath joined together, let not man put asunder'."

In his dairy, James quotes Dr Duncan where he says, "If only *convinced* sinners are warranted to come to Christ, then I must ere I can be warranted to embrace Him, be convinced that I am a convinced sinner. True, the convinced sinner is the only capable subject of saving faith, but it is not as a convinced sinner I am called upon to come to Christ. The Gospel does not address convinced sinners as such with offers of reconciliation, but *fallen* sinners. It is a very beautiful arrangement in the Gospel that it does not proclaim itself to *convinced* sinners."

— 1 —

In a diary-entry as late as December 1977 Mr Morrison recalls his constant astonishment, as a youth, at the note of deep penitence that he always detected in his grandfather's prayers. "In my young days in the faith," he writes, "When I was about 17 years, I used to be greatly affected by my dear and saintly grandfather's prayers. This impression however remained with me for many years before I could understand its context and logic. With the dew descending in the course of his prayer, his petitions and praises were most affecting; perhaps in the one prayer three or four separate moments of this kind were noticeable. At the same time this was a question to me, why on every one of these occasions he would refer to his sins and in broken accents make confession of them and pray against them. Some years passed then it was all understood; it was his knowledge of sin — his own sin — that was at work there. Every time he experienced the presence of the Lord he at once translated it into the accents of penitence and repentance; that was to him a special moment for the special purpose of undermining the power and pollution of his sin."

Throughout his Christian life James never lost his dread of superficiality in religion. Good works, however meritorious in the sight of men, must be given no place in our account with God. He writes: "I never wish to make any subjective, soul-enriching experience basic to my acceptance in the Lord, and foundational to my hope of grace and of glory for this is bound up with and ever related to the great atonement of the Lord Jesus Christ. What is *in* me is not the basis of what is *for* me, but what is *for* me in terms of doctrine must be *in* me or *upon* me in terms of righteousness by faith before I can inherit eternal life. How easy it is for us to lose our way here; to confuse things that differ; to favour the Arminian while we hold the Antinomian in disfavour! God ever be my defence and stay."

## 2

Like Bunyan's "Pilgrim", James Morrison's "Progress" was marked by stern conflict all along the way. The battles were severe, but the spoils were rewarding. "I am at times humble before God," he writes, "that my theology is that of the field of battle and not that of the divan of speculation and mental acrobatics. I learn the hard way and that *is* learning; for it never exists alone and so it never fosters pride and arrogancy."

And he adds: "I had a reflection today that stopped me for a while. In my young days what the Puritans called a 'Law Work' was the common experience of believers. I had it too, and in the intensity of it at the beginning, it was after the pattern of the Apostle Paul's experience. 'He was three days without sight, and neither did eat nor drink.' Today, however, there is hardly a reference to such experiences."

Backsliding, he believed, was often due to presumptuous self-reliance. Commenting on the stilling of the tempest, as narrated in Matthew, chapter 8, and quoting the Lord's reproof to the disciples, "Why are ye fearful, O ye of little faith?" He says: "The background here is very instructive (see v. 19). How many kirk-sessions in Scotland would have dealt with this scribe as He did? He faced him with the *cost* of discipleship. Verse 21 — here again Christ enlists the sympathy of this disciple with no fleshly hope of any kind. Instead He underlines at once a test of loyalties and His own claims to unqualified and enduring service from all His followers. The case of the disciples in the storm is of the same order. They followed Him always, but would they honour Him with their faith at all times? Surely, when He was aboard and asleep they should not fear! The waves and the seas were to Him a fit setting for rest and sleep. *But little faith is not capable of riding out a storm.* It was in virtue of His humanity that He slept, it was by the power of His Godhead that He stilled the waves and the sea."

## 3

James Morrison had passed through varied experiences since that unforgettable night — the night of his deliverance,

Rev. and Mrs Morrison *(see page 18)*.

Rev. J. Morrison and Mr Neil Cameron. Mr Cameron, a native of Uist, was Mr Morrison's Missionary-assistant in Grimsay for some years.

Rev. James Morrison, with three fellow-Councillors, awaiting arrival of Prime Minister Edward Heath

when — his friend — as he tells us later — had set him off "in a bit of a dance" in his beloved Scalpay. In the interval he had learned to say with Edward Mote,

> I dare not trust my sweetest frame,
> But wholly lean on Jesus' name.

Moreover, he had discovered that there are many things in the experience of the Christian that are not Christian experience. Among these were the doubts and fears that had so often caused him spiritual anguish. But even these were caught up in the "all things" that "work together for good to them that love God". They are made to serve as calls to prayer and incitements to thanksgiving. "How unresponsive my heart is in all God's great kindness," he writes, "in every case 'my heart hates my heart' as Mr Boston once put it. I felt my prayer at worship this morning was in brief: 'Lord let me live and not die'. *I dread the area of life in which I find that it is well-nigh impossible for me to pray against sin with my whole heart and mind;* when sin has, as it were, lined my heart and understanding with its attractions and power. As long as I am consciously able with no leakage in my determination to pray against it, I cherish some confidence that the battle is mine, though at the same time I am deeply conscious of the corruption of my whole nature in the entire conflict. That might appear morbid introspection to some — it might taste too much of a species of Arminianism to others. But it is neither. The sovereignty of God takes effect in and through such experiences in life."

As God used Israel's enemies to turn His wayward people back to Himself, so He uses these dark fears and doubts to bring His tried saints back to the audience chamber of the King to cast all their care upon Him and learn anew that the He careth for them.

It is of one of these audiences that Mr Morrison writes: "After I succeeded in measure to get to my knees the heavens dropped rain. In my case I had an experience of 'mercy rejoicing against judgment' in my life today, in both the noon and evening services."

And on another occasion: "Worship was somewhat stale and I had a stale day throughout. Indeed I don't know when

I have had such a meaningless day at all. I was kept down at every turn since I arose this morning. It was simply beyond me to read, to study, to pray or do anything to get me anywhere. I am simply bound after the pattern of Lazarus, bound hand and foot with graveclothes and my head bound up in a napkin. In his case, however, there was every hope of his having these things removed, for life throbbed through all his veins. In my case it is not so easy to cherish such a confidence, for I am not conscious of the least sign of life at work at all. How am I going to face my pulpit in this pagan frame of mind. I am, indeed, full of confusion. I phoned my dear friend, Kenneth, of Beauly, tonight. After he had quoted his texts for tomorrow, in answer to my question, I was scared he would ask for mine, for I was altogether drifting in a wide sea without landmarks of any kind. He didn't ask me and I was relieved. Before I fell off to sleep I landed on a word — in 1 Cor. 15, v. 4 — that deeply moved my sub-conscious mind, it referred me back to my sorrow of late — to dear Norman's end 'And he was buried'. There was another word that brought some refreshing for a moment 'Master, it is good for us to be here', Luke 9, v. 33.''

— 4 —

Sometimes, in the spiritual warfare, the battle seemed to go completely against him, and his faith was strained to breaking point. Only three years before his death he wrote: "Before rising from my bed today I sensed the corruption of my heart; nothing ever changes my flesh! However could I become an Arminian! But certain facts were underlined for me within a few moments; I could claim that I took God's side in all this; that in all conscious sincerity I did this against my own lusts and corruption as a whole. I am being schooled in this holy discipline in a special way of late years.''

In words like those that we have quoted, James reveals much of the background that made him the man he was. The roots of the religious community to which he belonged went deep. They were a people who drew near to God with

56

reverence and godly fear. Their critics spoke of their religion as gloomy; but the description merely reveals the incapacity of these critics to distinguish between gloominess and solemnity. Lionel Fletcher used to tell of a negro attendant on an American train with whom he had struck up a conversation in the course of a journey. The man was a professing Christian, and a mine of information regarding the religious life of the people of those parts. "Do they *enjoy* their religion?" asked Fletcher.

The accuracy of the answer was not matched by elegance of expression: "Them that has it does!"

Yes, *"them that has it"* — men and women who, like Bunyan's Christian, had been led by the Spirit to the place "somewhat ascending" upon which "stood a cross, and, a little below, in the bottom, a sepulchre" into which the burdens of their sin had disappeared from their sight. "He hath given me rest by His sorrow," said Christian, "and life by His death."

And "he stood still awhile to look and wonder". . . . He looked therefore, and looked again, even till the springs that were in his head sent the waters down his cheeks. Morbidness? So the more volatile fraternity would describe it; but they would be wrong. For there, Christian gave three leaps for joy, and went on his way *singing*

> "Blessed Cross! blessed sepulchre! blessed rather be
> The man that there was put to shame for me."

And *that* is the distinctive thing about Christian joy; the ever-intermingling elements of gladness and sadness as the believer relates his redemption to the price that procured it. And, far from lessening the gladness, the sadness gives it an exuberance that goes beyond all earthly joy, and hallows it, and gives it the quality of endurance that is indicated in the word spoken by Nehemiah to a penitent Israel, "the joy of the Lord is your strength".

James Morrison came to know all this in personal experience. Going back to his conversion, he writes: "The first night I was set free, after my worthy father had worship, I said to my mother 'I must not go to bed just now'. It was about 11.00 p.m. She in her own dear way replied 'Where can you go at this time of night?' There was no 'night beat' in those days. Well, I dressed and walked out of the house. On arriving at the end of the house I found J. M. waiting for me. 'I was,' he said, 'praying that you would come,' and he added, 'Norman and Miret heard you were set free and they wanted to see you.' That was a happy contact for dear Norman embraced me and set me off in a bit of a dance. He then advised his dear one to make a meal and, after this, to have worship together. I love to think of it all in that distant past. I was the lamb then.''

But the halcyon times of spiritual youth do not continue. Strength must be tried if it is to increase; faith must be tested if it is to develop; and there is much in James Morrison's diary to show that he was a Christian of deep exercise. The sluggishness of his soul was a constant concern to him.

''I went to bed last night,'' he writes in one place, ''more dead than alive. I could think of nothing more comparable to my condition than the sinful sleep of the disciples in the Garden of Gethsemane. At a time when man's hour and that of the power of darkness was enveloping the soul of the Son of Man, when so many sinners needed salvation, how unreasonable and wicked it was that the disciples should be asleep. That was the type of temptation I was bound up in.''

— 5 —

His study door gave him no protection from Satan's intrusions. ''I wasn't late in getting to my work,'' he writes of one Saturday morning, ''but I drifted along helplessly without rhyme or reason in any of my moods. I was kept free from the entanglements of the flesh in any form, but I went to bed at night without a message for my poor people. It was borne home to me, however, that I had been neglectful of certain exercises of late. One of the most precious sources of inspiration over the years was our morning and evening worship, and I was led to see that I had lost some of the finest breathings of heart in this exercise.''

The formality of which he complains became the immediate subject of prayer and re-dedication, and the enemy was routed.

There were times also when the order was reversed and a day that began well ended disappointingly. "I have been conscious," he writes, "of some indecisiveness of heart today, that I could not dilute or overturn at all; I verily think that I have the most traitorous heart that any human being can have in this world; it is a heart that can respond to anything except the truth as it is in Jesus. I was relieved somewhat in the consideration of the righteousness of one and the obedience of one as emphasised in Rom. 5: 18, 19; for that is the righteousness and the obedience which procure our salvation."

His dog, Jet, disappointed him one day by his perverted tastes, but, he reflected, in what respect was he any better himself?

"Our dog 'Jet' is treated as a member of this home. He gets sufficient to eat and to drink. He has a comfortable bed. But, notwithstanding all this — and perhaps because of it — I saw him of late actually wallowing in a load of rotten seaweed that I had secured for the garden. He was the dog even amid all his comforts and privileges."

Jet's master felt that he was no better than his dog in his tastes. But on reflection, he came to see that there was a difference after all; for whereas the dog found satisfaction in the gratification of its desires, the man cried out against his own baseness. "Once again," he testifies, "my cry to the Lord was one for forgiveness. My flesh! My flesh! My flesh! I am, indeed, made to realise that this is not my rest, for it is polluted; this is so from this negative side; it is so from the positive side also; for I have often of late a sense of pining to get away — a kind of homesickness for heaven. God, however, was my conscious help today, in enabling me to devote this day to Him in holy meditation.

Morning worship, on another occasion, was "somewhat off colour", but, at the same time, he adds, "it meant an unveiling of my heart. . . . Yes, it drew my attention to John 1: 8. 'If we say we have no sin . . . the truth is not in us.' It is easy to say that we have sin. It is not so easy to be conscious of it; to be pained by it. Well, that was my lot for the whole of this day; that the pleasure of the Lord was at work in having my flesh laid bare to the fire and to all other discomforts also.''

Another morning, he writes: ''Worship had fine thoughts for us this morning; yes, but how few find lodgment in my heart. I often fear that death may come without my heart being truly dedicated to the Lord. O that His Spirit might truly convince me of sin, of righteousness and of judgment to come! The spirit is indeed willing but the flesh is weak.'' He noted that ''the Beloved spoke first of their spirit (His disciples) as being *willing,* before He referred to their flesh as being *weak.*'' And the thought comforted him.

— 6 —

At his very worst, James Morrison was conscious of Divine upholding. On 26th August 1974, he tells us: ''It has of late given me much help that the 'malefactor' loved of the Lord was called, justified, sanctified and glorified in the one day. When I consider all that the Lord has done for me and in me all these years — since I professed His name in 1927 — and yet sense my remaining corruption, I know not what to say. But his grace is, sufficient and His strength is made perfect in weakness. Well I know my weakness; I am ever conscious of it; and I trust that I lean more heavily on the God of all grace as a result.''

In all his wrestling, faith always directed him to the right source of succour; as witness the following: ''Worship was an unveiling of my deceitful heart. Ah! yes, but it was *an endearing look in the direction of the empty tomb also.* For some time I seem to find greater comfort in what Christ accomplished once and for all than I have had for many years previously. For a time in the morning I was with the Puritan, Clarkson. 'The blood is not sprinkled once on the mercy-seat or seven times before it, as under the law; but that sprinkling which it signified is continued for ever; the blood of sprinkling, wherewith our high priest entered into the holy place, remains there eternally. . . . His intercession has the virtue of a continued, of an everlasting prayer'. The whole range of the Saviour's obedience partook of the infinitude of His person. Not one moment of His humiliation on behalf of men was lived but in virtue of His person. How solemnising; how soul-enriching and sanctifying this is!''

His frequent deep convictions of sin often dimmed his assurance of salvation. Looking back to his spiritual youth, he recalls: ''I was full of assurance of God's love to me and the Saviour's love to me also. Indeed I was so confident of this that I once said to a friend 'I would defy Satan himself to deprive me of this assurance.' But the scourgings of life have made my flesh so corrupt and so challenging to me that generally speaking, I am often a stranger to this assurance now.''

But the mood of fear was not left in unchallenged mastery. I have often trembled on the rock,'' says J. C. Ryle, *"but I have never felt the Rock tremble under me."*

James Morrison knew in personal experience what that meant. He had learned that "the just shall live by faith", and that the strength communicated through faith was nothing less than the power of God, which is perfected through weakness, and against which the attacks of even the gates of Hell shall be in vain. He loved the Reformed Faith because of this note of certainty which pervades it. In another diary entry, he writes: "I was deeply moved as I reflected on how the dear Reformers emphasised assurance as practically essential to salvation. Their newly-found faith was so consciously precious to them that such an accompaniment was, one might say, natural to them. This made me think of my own life in the distant past; of one day after a University examination while passing by Edinburgh Castle on my way to my lodgings. A fellow student — D. M. — asked me: 'James are you assured of your soul's salvation?' My immediate reply was 'Donald, I am so assured of it that I am persuaded that no power of Satan is able to deprive me of it'. I then added: 'I am not so assured of my call to the ministry; indeed I wish sometimes that I were taken up to heaven and if I had five minutes there I would ask God if He had chosen me for this work. On my receiving a favourable answer I would then come back to earth to face any hardship for the Gospel'. What a change set in, in the case of the next generation of Reformers; what a change set in with me too!''

The frequent assaults that Mr Morrison endured upon his faith had the effect of making him a tender pastor, well equipped ''to speak a word in season to him that is weary''. When he got a word for himself he shared it with others in the hope that it would help them too. ''I read today extracts from the life of Billy Bray. 'All my life,' said Billy, 'I have had to take vinegar and honey. But praise the Lord, I have had to take the vinegar with a salt-spoon — but He has given the honey with a ladle!' I could make that confession also, and the mystery of it will remain with us so long as we know only in part. The very Captain of our Salvation was made perfect through suffering.''

Never, even at the worst, is he envious of the prosperity of the wicked. ''The believer, at his lowest ebb,'' he writes, ''is eternally and gloriously different from the sinner at his highest and best. A living dog is better than a dead lion. Nothing is little that commands the blessing of the triune Jehovah; nothing is big that commands His curse. Well, I know that I am a sinner but I trust I know Christ too — and even better. May He grant that Ps. 121 will all be realised in my experience.''

The message of this Psalm had been a constant source of blessing to him over the years. On New Year's Day, 1970, he writes: ''It was a reminder of olden days — of the days of my first love. It set me back to that holy night in which my bonds were set free and I kept awake all night. What conscious peace and joy filled my heart! The word that God applied principally to my case was Ps. 121: 1. I was led to this precious experience in the service today but, of course, I quoted it without any personal reference whatsoever.''

I once quoted in his hearing the words of C. H. Spurgeon, ''Brethren, be great believers, and ye shall be great receivers. Small faith will indeed bring your souls to heaven, but great faith will bring heaven to your souls.'' He smiled his appreciation, and repeated the quotation afterwards. "Good advice," he remarked. "The Lord help us to act upon it."

The following extract from the diary seems to suggest that the needed help was sought and given: "Lately I have been dwelling more on assurance especially this high spiritual attainment in John's letters: 1 John 1: 2 — "We have *seen . . . bear witness* and *shew* unto you". Verse 3 — *"truly* our fellowship is with the Father and with His Son Jesus Christ". "Behold what manner of love . . . that we should be called *the sons of God"*. Ch. 3: 2 — *"now are we the sons of God."* And, despite our present deformity, "we shall yet be like Him".

It was in this great thought that Merle D'Aubigne, the historian of the Reformation, found relief in his youth. While a student at Kiel, he was sorely oppressed with doubts, and sought out a deeply experienced Christian to help him answer them. But the old consultant refused help along those lines. "Were I to rid you of these fears," he said, "others would soon fill their place. There is a shorter way of destroying them. Let Christ be to you really the Son of God — the Saviour — and His light will dispel the darkness, and His Spirit lead you into all truth."

In Christ's Sonship, the great French divine, found release from his fear, and the comfort of being himself, through Christ, a son of God.

— 8 —

It may be that, at times, Mr Morrison's dread of shallowness made him over-cautious in his dealings with people showing signs of religious concern. He would have approved the reproof spoken by Dr James Kidd of Aberdeen, to John Duncan when, together, they were visiting a condemned criminal in his prison cell. John Duncan was a student at the time, and with all the eagerness of youth was interspersing his Bible-reading in the prison cell with rambling comments of his own in which he seemed, to Dr Kidd, to be pressurising the criminal with more zeal than prudence into an acceptance of the Gospel. "Young man," broke in Dr Kidd, "will you hold your tongue, and let the Holy Ghost speak?"

James Morrison would have understood, as, indeed, John Duncan did when he reflected on his pastor's words. James was ardently supportive of evangelistic effort, but regarded the excessive pressurism, which is so much a feature of modern evangelism, as contrary to the deepest interests of the persons dealt with in this fashion. He notes a reference which appears in the *Memoirs of Adolph Saphir* (page 18), and copies it into his diary as indicative of his own thinking: "I am sorry to say the first Jew who was influenced by Moody has relapsed into unbelief. We are very much grieved and must continue praying for his restoration and conversion. I fear there is much superficial work at meetings and too great hurry to get people to say they have peace, also comforting people who have no sorrow or burden."

— 9 —

The diary makes it fully evident that Mr Morrison too had serious misgivings about modern mass-evangelism. The greatest Evangelist of all had often spoken warningly about "counting the cost", and in His parable of the Sower had revealed the fate of the seed growing in "stony places" — a clear warning against shallowness in religion. In his own life, and throughout his ministry, Mr Morrison echoed that warning. Like Joseph Alleine, he was "insatiably greedy of souls", but he looked askance at the pressurising methods of some modern evangelists. He was not misled by the exuberance generated at some of these mass meetings, and deplored the high rate of spiritual casualty that too often resulted from the drive for "decisions".

There came to my hands recently a copy of the Moderatorial Address given by the Rev. George Mackay, of Fearn, to the Free Church General Assembly of 1923 — an address described by Dr Alexander Stewart as being — "whether regarded from the viewpoint of matter, or literary form, or method of delivery among the best ever heard in that Assembly Hall". I was there as a student when it was delivered, and the thrill of that hour was awakened anew in me when, half a century later, I read it in print.

There were revival movements in Scotland at the time, and some of them were causing concern because of the absence of conviction of sin and true repentance among many of the listed converts. Mr Mackay, a warm-hearted and greatly used evangelist himself, felt moved to sound a note of caution. The temptation to quote him is irresistible.

"There are two elements in the Cross," he declared, "Love and Righteousness, and neither should overshadow the other. That there have been remarkable religious movements associated with a presentation of the Cross in which the Love of God has been made to eclipse His righteousness cannot be denied, but allow me to say as one who has come in contact with religious movements, commonly called 'revivals', that such a presentation of the Cross, as I now refer to, is not Apostolic, and the type of religious experience produced by such a presentation does not represent the imperial vein of Christian experience from the days of the Apostles downwards. There is usually little of any 'law work', no apprehension of any reality of guilt, no really searching crisis of self-adjustment before a holy God, no dying to oneself and becoming alive unto God, no brokenness of heart and contrition of spirit, no gentle gladness of the healed and wondering soul, but no lack of the boisterousness of unbroken self-confidence. To quote a dictum of that greatly-blessed servant of the Lord, the Rev. A. Douglas Brown, whose name is a household word in all our fishing villages on the north-east of Scotland — 'Revival', says he, 'is not going down the street with a big drum, it is going back to Calvary with a big sob'."

That fear of superficiality never left James Morrison. His longing for conversions breaks out again and again in these daily jottings, but nothing would ever induce him to apply pressure. A modern Christian writer tells of a little girl who was once found by her mother in the garden, squeezing the rose-buds. "Stop, stop, Margaret", cried her mother. "whatever are you doing?" And Margaret, sensing disapproval, replied defensively, "O, mother, I was just helping God to open the rose-buds".

There are evangelists, over-eager for decisions, and professions of conversion, who make the same mistake. Nature takes its own time to open out the hidden glory of the rose, and the Holy Spirit works to His own plan in bringing men and women to a saving knowledge of Christ, and a public profession of His Name.

But wherever Mr Morrison detected even the beginnings of a quickened interest in spiritual things his whole heart went out in prayer for the person or persons concerned. To be the means of bringing, or helping, a soul to Christ — the world itself could offer no greater honour, nor bestow a richer reward.

In conversation with James on the way home from church on one occasion, I referred to a man who was showing concern regarding the duty of making public profession of the name of Christ. James believed that the man had indeed passed through a spiritual crisis but was not yet ready for that decisive step. "I'm praying for him every day," he said, "and I strongly believe that the Lord will give him to us yet."

The next time I was at communion services in North Uist it was evident that Mr Morrison had a real burden on his heart for this diffident disciple. He felt that if he did not come forward at that communion he might never come at all. At every time of family worship he remembered him in prayer. When he came home from his Kirk Session meeting on Saturday he was radiant. His friend had appeared before them to profess his faith in Christ and to seek admission to His Table. That communion service had a very special joy for Mr Morrison and, inevitably, it was given special mention in his diary jottings for the day.

"It did my soul good to have experienced this," he writes, "He has done me much good in the work of the Lord over many years; so it seems he has decided in the name of the Lord to enlist in the Army of the Lord."

The seed sown where there is "deepness of earth" to receive it takes longer to send its tender shoots through the covering soil into the light and warmth of the sunshine above, in contradistinction from the seed which fell upon "stony places" where there was not much earth; but it was the seed in the deep soil that endured the scorching heat of summer, and "brought forth fruit, some an hundred-fold, some sixty-fold, some thirty-fold".

Which things are indeed "an allegory".

# CHAPTER EIGHT

## REST AND RECREATION

**The Reaper is equally paid even for the time in which he sharpens his sickle.**
—THOMAS GOODWIN.

Mr Morrison did not allow himself a regular annual holiday, and when he did take a few days off, it was certainly not in the spirit of a Skye "Moderate" of long ago who, when he boarded the Kyle steamer at Portree, dropped his suitcase on the deck and remarked, with unconcealed satisfaction, to a fellow-traveller of like ecclesiastical persuasion, "Now, no more preaching or praying for me for a whole month!"

To James Morrison the supreme luxury of life was preaching the Gospel of Christ, setting forth the unsearchable riches of His grace, and beseeching sinners in His stead, to be reconciled to God. Everything else was incidental. Throughout his ministry he enjoyed good health, and rest periods seemed almost a waste of precious time. Indeed, one gets the impression that such holidays as he did take were taken for the sake of his "dear one", as he almost invariably designates his wife, for Mrs Morrison did not share his quality of robustness, nor the blessing of regular and deep sleep, the "sleep that knits up the ravell'd sleave of care". There are various hints in the diary that holidays were taken for her benefit rather than his own.

— 1 —

The prospect of worship and congenial Christian fellowship had much to do with the selection of the holiday quarters. If there was a Free Church congregation nearby, the Morrisons naturally made their temporary spiritual home there. In other areas, particularly south of the Border, they sought out the nearest evangelical congregation and made many friends among them.

Holidays that gave them special enjoyment are given extended mention. One of these was at Broughty Ferry in 1967, where they had the welcome opportunity of becoming acquainted with the Free Church in Dundee. The Session Clerk, Major W. M. Mackay, was already known to James, for the Major was for many years Convener of the Finance, Law and Advisory Committee of the Free Church, and a prominent figure in the General Assembly. Both men were keen Celts with a common interest in Church History and Theology — and Gaelic! Of an afternoon in Dundee James writes:

"29th August 1967. In the afternoon we left for Dundee. We had tea with Major Mackay. When he took me to his library I asked him if he ever saw any of Bush's works. He replied: 'I have him on Genesis'. That was the very thing I searched for during these last 15 years. He gave me this book on loan for a year. God led me to this — I feel assured that this was so. We had a time of blessing together. He showed us the Wishart Arch — where George Wishart, the martyr, preached when the plague visited Dundee. It was a moving experience to see it — and it is a great blessing that the event is still remembered. Home here at 9 p.m. God filled in our time today with many ingredients of blessing."

"30th August: Major Mackay — our worthy elder in Dundee — called for us at 9.30 a.m. and took us to St Andrews. It was a solemn day. We visited Samuel Rutherford's grave. He and Thomas Halyburton lie side by side in the old cemetery. Just like the corruption their bodies are meantime shrouded in, so their dust is encompassed about with the relics of abominable Popery. Visited the Bottle Dungeon in the Castle, and the underground tunnel — the work of Protestants at the one end and the work of the Pope's emissaries at the other. What "marks of the beast' are seen there! And the Churches we visited are gradually falling in line with the tendencies and principles that produced such a harvest of evil in the Church in Scotland and elsewhere. The Reformers are kept in memory not to enhance the faith of our fathers but to underline the grave injustices executed on popish sophistries and satanic

69

idolatries; that is the type of presentation made of our Covenanters and martyrs nowadays. But we had a very profound message from it all. Arrived back at 4.30 p.m. Crossed by train at 5.43 p.m. Took prayer meeting. Text: Mt. 26: 1-2. Bus home at 9.40 p.m. Blessing on this day.''

"31st August: Called on a Mr Elis, who took me to see his garden. Mrs Elis made tea for us. They are Baptists, and we enjoyed their fellowship. The Gospel makes for naturalness and courtesy as well as for the higher virtues. Met Mr Douglas Milne by appointment there. He is a prospective student of our Church. He took us to St Peter's Church — where the saintly Robert Murray McCheyne was once minister. I stood in his pulpit and endeavoured to pray there — with my dear wife and Mr Milne. How touching it all was! Looked into his Bible also — with its blank-leaved notes. God make me worthy of all this past! Arrived home at 5 p.m. Remainder of night spent in peace and quietness. God was our help all day.''

— 2 —

Another of these short holidays was spent at Ayr, where the late Rev. Kenneth Taylor was then exercising his gracious ministry in Martyrs' Free Church.

"One of my concerns in coming to Ayr was lest I should be so far from the Church that I should have to use transport to get there. But the Church was actually only a ten minutes' walk from our quarters. Mr Taylor gave us a good word on the fig tree which the Lord cursed. He is a warm-hearted and cultured type of preacher. The attendance was quite good in the morning, but the evening was not so good. I felt a very good and healthy type of atmosphere about the congregation. They took us to their hearts and that was a great encouragement to us. God grant us to be worthy of such friends always and everywhere. It is a priceless privilege to share in such fellowship.''

The special interest that attached to Ayr as a holiday resort for the Morrisons was that it was on the edge of Scotland's Covenanting Martyrland. Mr Taylor took them to several places of interest; to Ayrsmoss, where young

In the garden (left to right): Rev A. Montgomery, Professor Collins
and Rev. J. Morrison *(see page 77)*.

Rev. K. Macleay, Rev. K. MacRae and Rev. J. Morrison *(see pages 79, 80)*.

Rev. James Morrison and Rev. Peter Fraser on Grampian Ski-lift
*(see page 92).*

Richard Cameron shed his blood for his faith; to Fenwick, where William Guthrie's old Church is surrounded by martyr graves; to Lochgoin, where so many Covenanters found refuge in the home of John Howie in days of persecution; and, most memorable of all, to Wigton, the scene of the martyrdom, by drowning in the Solway, of Margaret Lauchlison and young Margaret Wilson. They went out to the monument marking the site of the stake where young Margaret was drowned, and visited the place where the two martyrs are buried.

"We had prayer at the grave — each of us in turn," James recalls: "I felt a sweet unction in the exercise. On our way back from the stake which marks approximately the place where Margaret Wilson gave her young life to the Lord, we met a young father and his three-year-old daughter going there. Her name was Sarah. I left a word of encouragement with her and her father. What instruction this day had for me! How true it was in this case that the 'name of the wicked shall rot' while at the same time the 'memory of the righteous shall be blessed' — or, literally, 'for a blessing'. That was the message of this day to me. We also had a time of blessing in the car."

— 3 —

James Morrison and his friend Kenneth Macleay, minister of the Free Church in Beauly and Strathglass, had long planned a holiday on the uninhabited island of Heisker, and in 1966 it came to pass. James would probably have reckoned Kenneth his most intimate friend outside his family circle. The bond between the two men, formed in student days, seemed to grow stronger with the passing years. They were frequently in each other's Manses, and were very much of the same mind and outlook in matters theological and ecclesiastical. And they both loved the sea, for Kenneth had seen service with the Anchor-Donaldson Line before studying for the ministry. His trip to Heisker was the fulfilment of a long-cherished hope. They were to sail on Monday, 15th August, and this necessitated Kenneth's presence in North Uist over the weekend.

71

F

James takes up the story.

"13th August: Late in going to bed — Mr Kenneth and I. But sleep after it was sweet. Discussed various things during the day. He is weighted against the uncharted tendencies of this hour, and in favour of the sure mercies of David — the whole counsel of God as revealed to us in the Word and in our Church Confessions and Orders. God ever win my whole heart in unreserved allegiance and devotion to the Reformed Faith — the only true Faith. And this should in turn find expression in the things we say, as well as the things we do not say; the things we do, as well as the things we do not do. We should be good citizens, 'render to Caesar the things that are Caesar's'. We should be charitable, and give to Christian and social institutions. We should be hospitable — all of us should imitate Abraham and Sarah — Gen. 18: We should encourage the highest integrity in business; and the fear of God in employer-employee relationships. And we should beware of covetousness."

"14th August: Sabbath. We had a truly spiritual worship today. Dear Kenneth loves Uist — loves it for the sake of those I love, and he is loved in turn for that reason. He preached an able and edifying sermon today. Text: Heb. 11: 13-14. Our people were truly refreshed. He took Sollas for me at 3 p.m. and he preached here again at night. We had the Lord's covering all day. At worship we prayed for this to continue with us all week — in all things and everywhere."

"15th August: Left at 2.30 p.m. for Gramsdale — to join Grimsay fishermen. Left for Heisker at 5 p.m. Crossing was uncomfortable enough, but we were in good form for a meal when we arrived. Right there and then His care for us appeared. Charles Stewart, Kallin, invited us to take his room, which was in splendid condition — lino on floors, calor-gas light and two rings for cooking; locker with sliding doors for food, etc. We had worship every night with the young men there. They all gathered together into William Macinnes' room. There were ten of us altogether and we experienced God's blessing there from the start."

"16th August: Day was very windy and showery. We didn't make the sea of it today. All the fishermen were kept at home, but we turned the day to good account. And my good friend, Kenneth, thinks the change is doing him good. May it prove a real and lasting blessing to him. I can always endeavour to pray with this dear brother. Worship at night was again uplifting and solemnising."

"17th August: Slept much better last night — Heisker is telling on Kenneth more and more. The Atlantic ozone is more pungent in his case, for he is not so acclimatised to it on the east coast as I am here on the west. He slept better in any case. We strolled along the beaches today. The day was warm and very pleasant. We had prayer together, too. God's presence was very real and precious to us this whole afternoon. All the fishermen were at their work today. They were doing well. God bless them ever and always. I feel so happy that these young men, all from my own Congregation, are at the work that their fathers and grandfathers and great grandfathers were at. The earth abides forever; and so does the sea. The Gospel is always a producer, protector and sustainer of commonsense. And the livelihood these boys are pursuing is one of commonsense."

"18th August: We accompanied the fishermen to sea today. Mr Kenneth joined the Mackinnon boys, while I went off with the Nicolson, Baymore, boy. We had a very good day's fishing. And he was very glad to have me with him for there was quite a swell running and he had his creels in somewhat exposed places. We have rare feasts of lobsters, crabs, winkles, etc. And my good friend Kenneth, beats me in this as in other things. He has a voracious appetite for lobsters!"

"19th August: Started off with fishermen again and in the same boats. Had a lovely day at sea and good catches. Nicolson and I went fishing with cast — only four hooks, however. What a haul we had of young saithe, lythe, mackerel, etc. We cleaned saithe in the sea, boiled it at once and had it for lunch. But Kenneth preferred his cold lobsters with the potatoes. Set off at 6 p.m. to visit other crews in the West end of Heisker. Had tea with Roderick Stewart, and Kenneth and I experienced a special blessing on it. In the grace at the beginning and at the giving of thanks there was a clear indication of the Lord's presence with us. It was a day of manifold blessings.''

"20th August: Glorious day. Set off for Grimsay at 10.20 a.m. Had a lovely meal in Charles Stewart's home. God blessed us all week. I have had no regrets in it all. Mr Kenneth will have all day in Grimsay tomorrow. He initiated the visit to Heisker with a holy and acceptable ministration here and he will conclude it all with a similar blessing. He is able to make contact with the finest and best here.''

The long-awaited Heisker holiday had, quite evidently, come up to expectations. The fellowship had been congenial; the exertions exciting, and the rest sweet. Reminiscently, James remarks, "I thought of my dear father. He used to say, 'Two hours sleep at sea is to me the equivalent of seven hours sleep anywhere else'.''

And James agreed.

— 4 —

Returning home from a holiday spent in the South on another occasion, it was proposed to Mr Morrison that they might travel from Troon to Scalpay by Roderick Cunningham's boat, *Isle of Lewis*. The prospect had a strong appeal, and James tells us the rest.

"My wife and I laid the matter before the Lord and we both were fully convinced that this was the course to follow. We accompanied Sandy to St Enoch, and joined the 12.30 p.m. train to Troon. We left for Scalpay at 2.20 p.m. Gale, severe, reported but we had a lovely evening. Had potatoes and herring for dinner, cold ham and salad for tea. And in betweens all the way. Mr Roddy himself was in good form. We were on bridge till 10.00 p.m. Crew joined us at worship. It was a real treat. We went to bed at 11.15 p.m. Run all day was very pleasant. Some swell going round Mull of Kintyre, but it did not affect us — not even Annie, my wife. Whole climate, all evening and night, was spiritual.''

Next morning: "Awakened refreshed. Sleep was precious aboard. We had a lovely bed. Gave Annie her breakfast in bed. I had mine with Roddy and Sandy. When I looked out about 8.00 a.m. we were nearing Rhum and Canna. It was a fine, bright morning. God was making us glad. How we enjoyed the run along the South end of Skye!''

"The tangle of the Isles?" Yes, but there was more to it than that, and James has let us into the secret.

There was an Unseen Presence on board the *Isle of Lewis* who warmed the hearts of a like-minded company, comprising crew and passengers, as they joined in the praises of their Saviour and Lord. And for Mr and Mrs Morrison, there was the lure of home. He writes: "No place like Uist". "This is graven on my heart for ever. It was sweet to see the light in my study once again; it was sweet to see it in the neighbourhood also. We bowed our knees on arriving to praise His name for all His mercies since we left home until our return."

While spending a few days in Fort William, with his kinsman, Rev. John Morrison, James sampled the holiday delights of Lochaber. Reviewing the events of one of these days in particular he writes: "I wakened to a lovely day. Worship seemed to mirror the day's prospects of blessing for me. We had, to begin with a fine run in the *Maid of Bute* skippered by my Aunt's son, Angus Macsween — a worthy member of his family. The outing was good in terms of both worlds. It had a very solemn lesson for me. Angus had made thousands of pounds out of runs to 'Seal rock'. He simply encircles the rock two or three times, to let his passengers see the seals, young and old basking in the sun. My rebuke was this: 'Am I so ready to utilise the solemn opportunities and privileges that are mine to do business for the Master, as this young man has done in harnessing nature to reap a rich harvest from it? I am afraid that I have again and again failed to rise to the height of things in this respect. The blood of Jesus Christ His Son, cleanse me from all sin! I have recourse to it at all times.'"

— 5 —

The lure of the sea never weakened for Mr Morrison. I had never seen it so much in evidence as when I was with him at Grimsay communion in July 1974. We were staying with the MacInnes family at Kallin, "this hospitable home" as Mr Morrison so truly describes it. "Yes," he proceeds, "it was as I said in Church, that if the prophet of old had blessing upon blessing showered upon him in the Shunamite home, so had we in *this home overlooking a bay and a sea I know so well and love even more.* Today's worship was His own and ours. And the service was, indeed, excellent from beginning to end. And God was over us; in us; with us; for us and ministered all good through His servant."

— 6 —

A holiday spent at Whitley Bay provided a variety of interests. His impressions of the resort are revealing, and they show why tourism was not his favourite industry.

"Beautiful day. Walked through main street before lunch. Called in shop for some collars. First time I wore ordinary collars for many years now, but I have never been to a place like this, nor had a holiday like this, before. Gentlemen in shop, Bolton of Whitley Bay, were very interesting. Guessed they were good conservatives. Took a walk round to see various Churches. Had to make a search before we found them. This in itself is a parable. This place appears to have been the product of tourism. Houses have something garish, unsubstantial about them. Old Parish Church has, indeed, the usual Victorian culture about it. And in keeping with this it occupies a prominent place in the Town — the Town as it was in Victorian times. Nearly all the houses are of a piece, representative of a middle class society and all, or nearly all, worshipping the mammon of tourism. Bought four secondhand issues of *Science of Thought Review* at 2d. each!"

"Last Sabbath we never moved out of doors, except to Church Service at 10.45 a.m. Baptist Church. Mr Middlemas's text: "*Speak to the Rock*". He referred to Moses' sin in terms of traditionalism, bitterness, refusal. God had said — not *smite* — but *speak.* Sermon was thoughtful and solid. Text in the evening: John 12: 26: *"him will my Father honour"*. He referred to various wordly honours; academical honour. He quoted hospital case where a brilliant academic brain was reduced to nil. Spoke of

76

business progression, political fame, sporting laurels, military, glory etc; but the honour that comes from God is greater. Very sound teaching here. Regretted that the Psalmody was second class. Grieved too that so many women attended without any head covering whatsoever."

"Monday, not so bright today. Must refer here to another Sabbath in Whitley Bay. The congregation listened well while the Minister, Mr Moore, from Edgehill College, Ormskirk, read the Scriptures. But eye-gate should be open here in addition to ear-gate. Five deacons took up the offering and placed it on the table right in front of pulpit — an altar and sacrifice in miniature. How like the uncircumcised ear and heart all this is! And the minister prayed in line with all this offence. Attended Baptist Church at night. Minister: Mr Middlemas. Text — John 12: 26. He was good. Emphasised new birth. Alive to danger of self righteousness. Two deacons placed offering on table here also. But prayer underlined danger involved in this. But why this stumbling block at all! Service here had a measure of life and warmth in it, but it lacked the dignity of the Presbyterian Church. Where there is fear towards God there is honourable dignity."

"Had a short walk in forenoon. Weather somewhat showery and cold today. At 11.30 we arrived at Jewish Synagogue at the end of Whitley Street. Encouraged to enter. Asked, however, to worship apart. My wife was placed among the ladies. I had to stand apart in the men's section. Irreverence characterised the whole worship. They whispered to one another, made signs to one another and even smiled across to the ladies while at the same time engaged in their devotions. It was a special example of calling on God with the lips and the heart far from Him. But there was an interesting simplicity about it. The Word was there — in the letter, of course. I was able to follow most of it, when the Order of the service was shown me. I noticed that they all looked somewhat untidy about the face. I asked one of the men if they shaved on Sabbath. 'No, No,' he replied. I informed him that I also never shaved on our Sabbath. Learned much in this contact."

But, wherever he went, Mr Morrison found a restfulness and peace in the Western Isles that no other place could match. Of a late holiday in Lewis he writes: "Enjoyed quietness and solitude down at 26 Branahuie. If ever I have a period of retirement I will make choice of a quiet corner by the sea, without the noise of cars in my ears or a sight of any such thing if that is at all possible. I have had such experiences of the ingratitude of man; of the superficiality of this generation; their madness for sport and entertainment, that I desire earnestly to have my end away from it all — if He wills it so."

*A quiet corner by the sea. . . .* That was his choice. There he would be among the people whom he loved most, and to whom he could open his heart without reserve. And there he would have every facility for his favourite/recreation, fishing. And what a master hand he was! On the occasion of my very first visit to him we spent an afternoon and evening fishing in shallow waters off Grimsay. It was lovely weather, and our labour was not in vain. Not that I contributed much to the catch. "They are all around you," shouted James encouragingly, with reference to the fish.

"I can sense that," I shouted back. "They know that it is safer at this end of the boat!" At all events, they nibbled at my bait with very little loss to themselves, but woe to the fish that ventured to take liberties with James's hooks! The erstwhile fishermen knew all the tricks of the trade!

Lobster-fishing was not so exciting, but he thrilled to that occupation also. Writing up his diary on a September morning, he says, "What a tonic yesterday's sea-trip proved to be! And I did a bit to help with the lifting of the creels too." And, later: "I rose up early to accompany my sister's boy to sea, to lift 350 creels set for lobsters in Loch Brollum. Before they finished I asked to be put ashore in the small harbour there that I knew so well as a boy, when I fished in the same way with my late dear grandfather and his brother Angus. How every corner of that coastline spoke to my heart; yes, to my heart, both as a human being and as a saved sinner in the name of the Lord! The effect of this on me was such that it made me wonder if it was not in the nature of a farewell that this experience was given me.''

Another recreation, which almost rivalled fishing, was gardening. "Who loves a garden," declares William Cowper, "loves a greenhouse too." And James Morrison had both, and loved both. The garden came first. There was ample scope for horticultural interests around the Bayhead Manse, and, properly cultivated, the land could supply the Manse table with vegetables for a good part of the year. James saw the value of such an amenity in a place like North Uist and decided — though not with much enthusiasm to begin with — to add it to his perquisites. But that was easier said than done. The land selected had to be brought into proper cultivation, and that meant hard work, and much of it. But as he toiled, with such assistance as was offered, his interest in the work grew, and soon became an enthusiasm. Here was a recreation that could be taken up at spare time. It was right at the door, and it gave a good return for the toil and money expended upon it. When the greenhouse was added the gardener's satisfaction with his new acquisition exceeded all his expectations. Here was a place where he could carry out his horticultural experiments even in wet and stormy weather. The transformation of the wilderness and solitary place proceeded apace. A riot of colour appeared in the extended flowerbeds. Plants raised from seed in the greenhouse grew to sturdy maturity under the skilled hand of the gardener. Fruit bushes contributed their own yield to the Manse table in due season. And not content with these environmental improvements, Mr Morrison constructed an artificial pool at the Manse gate, beautifying it with aquatic plants, and even stocking it with goldfish! It was a complete triumph. The Manse garden produce was unsurpassed in the Island; indeed, seldom equalled. And James made no secret of the cause of his success. Basically, it was using the right type of fertiliser. He would lecture his visitors by the hour on the subject. Artificial fertilisers he could not abide! Their very plastic containers stirred his disdain! Sea-weed, laced with the natural manure of their byres and stables; that was what was needed, and it was easily obtainable! Give *that* to the soil, and your recompense would be evident to all! And how could you rebut arguments that were supported by giant cabbages, and cauliflowers, and lettuces, and leeks, and onions, and carrots, and, perhaps most of all, turnips! "Last week," he records in one entry, "the Missionary and I lifted the last three turnips from the garden. The scales in the Manse — for 15 lbs. — could not cope with the largest of them. The Missionary went to the Post Office with it and it was put on the scales and weighed 19 lbs. 12 ozs. . . . ''

References to the garden, and the lessons that he learned there, come quite frequently into the diary. Here are some.

"I rose early for work in the garden. At worship I had an audience with the King, and in emerging from it I was convinced that the Lord was to administer all my affairs today. And He did. To begin with I began work on site preparation for my greenhouse; He enabled me to overtake this. The foundation is clear, and ready for the concrete when I get further help."

"Good day but somewhat cold. Worked in garden again — weeded in garden plot. The ground is like the human heart. It all looks so innocent and pure till one knows its nature and we begin to dig, to get at things below the surface. What a mass of competitiors are there, ready to start a race with the finest and best put into the soil by us. Perhaps a military figure is more to the point. The curse on and in the ground is in the form of trained soldiers ready to stab to death any and every form of precious life we confront them with; and just as we prepare different flowers and vegetables to appear in their respective months, so this curse has its destructive agents for every month too. No sign of chickweed at present. Nor of groundsel either. But their day has not come yet. They are reservists to be called up in July and August."

Again: "I was in the garden for a while in the forenoon and it was a real help to me. What a lesson that garden is! It is just what I would like the Church to be — God and the souls of all in sweetest harmony. That is what the literal garden and its throbbing life underlines, for every vegetable and plant are in the finest partnership with their whole environment. Indeed what nature always relishes is the fitness of things. And that is what is so evident in my garden. No ingredient is missing anywhere."

And still later: "I had a fine time in the garden. Between mint and certain types of daffodils and bushes — flowering currants, etc. I was again and again reminded of the sweet fragrance of the mountains of spices. And the birds were about me and ceaselessly making melody in my ears. God is over all, not in the flameless vision of the Pantheist and the Deist, but in very truth in Christ reconciling the world unto Himself."

"I learn something valuable in the garden every day. Hardly a moment but there is some life to be seen in it. But in the garden of the Lord there is fruit every month. Work of sanctification is always in progression."

— 9 —

For some years, Mr Morrison allowed himself a few days off duty in order to attend the annual Leicester Conference, for he found great enjoyment in meeting with the Reformed Christian leaders from many parts of the country, and from lands abroad, and to share with them the lectures arranged under the Banner of Truth Trust. James was an isleman without being insular. Scalpay and North Uist were, of course, quite special places, and he besought special blessing for them; but not in the spirit of a Millport parish minister of long ago whose invariable prayer for his island parish was that God would "bless the Greater and Lesser Cumbraes, and the adjacent islands of Great Britain and Ireland". When James prayed "Thy Kingdom come" he was really claiming the world for Christ, and was always avid for news of the spread of the Gospel in this and other lands.

He had met Dr Martyn Lloyd-Jones in 1939, when the Doctor delivered a series of lectures in the Free Church College, and immediately became his ardent disciple, frequently travelling considerable distances to hear him during the Doctor's many visits to Scotland. It is a safe guess that James's first visit to Leicester was motivated by the desire to deepen acquaintance with him as the Conference might make possible. "First time I heard Dr Lloyd-Jones," he recalls, "was in 1939. I cherished the conviction in the first lecture I ever heard from him that he would never disappoint me, and so it has been. God spare him for many years."

The Doctor's books were added to his well-stocked shelves as they made their appearance.

"For a period this evening," he writes in December 1973, "I sat at the feet of Dr Martyn Lloyd-Jones as I relished his teaching in his book on Romans, chapter 5. This is theology in the field; theology related to life and its conflicts; theology addressing itself to all the keys of the human organ — not only to the brain but also to the finest and best in human hearts everywhere. The fustiness of the museum is never present with this princely treatment of the Scriptures. Referring to trials and tribulations, he says that 'they always differentiate between what we can describe as believism', or 'fideism and true faith'. The man who merely has this kind of believism is found to fail altogether when the trials and tribulations come."

And, like Samson, having found his honeycomb and tasted its sweetness he desired to share it with his friends.

"I have completed an arrangement," he writes, "which provides for a copy of Dr M. Lloyd-Jones *Daily Readings* to be sent to every fishing-boat in Scalpay."

Another Leicester favourite was Professor John Murray, formerly of Westminster Theological Seminary, U.S.A. "Professor Murray is a Scotsman and a Celt," he comments; "He is independent, resourceful and Calvinistic in his theology. But he questions the scripturalness of the term 'invisible church'. Example of this speculative itch in America."

British Evangelicals also came under reproof.

"Noted in the case of the different branches of evangelicals that they had one thing in common, and in contrast with the Church of England and our own Presbyterianism. There was an absence of dignity, not to say an irreverence, in their approaches to God. Certain practices — posture in prayer, etc. — did not seem to enter their thoughts at all."

"Worship was a help today. It solemnised my spirit. That is a quality I am anxious to cultivate and further. In my student days in Edinburgh, I for a period stayed with one of the Caretakers in the City Chambers. On more than one occasion during our stay, Royalty dined in the City Chambers. I was informed by one of the officials that he always noticed the differences between Royalty and all the other guests. And one of the differences he emphasised was the dignity and gravity of their bearing. That is how Christians should be different too, in their bearing as King's sons and King's daughters."

"Evening service was again conducted by Mr A. Martin, from America. What a lovely word he gave us tonight! It was all in tune with the most profound exegesis of Scripture. God bless these young people who have come here. May it prove to us all a little reviving in our bondage. We have ministers here, and their wives and families. We have doctors, dentists, a lawyer, teachers, engineers, business-men of high standing, etc. God has called us all together to represent Him in all our varied capacities."

"This day was the Lord's in very truth. I noticed that most of our English friends wandered around quite a bit in the afternoon. They haven't had the same teaching regarding Sabbath Observance as we have had. But I am certain our Scottish emphasis is the right one — that the Day should be kept as free as possible from all recreation and worldliness and devoted to Him in its entirety. May He make me worthy of this Day's many blessings."

"Prayer meeting this morning was a real help again. We don't take part, because we are not of their persuasion in this method. They pray publicly without being called upon, and one or two women took part."

But where the message was true to the Evangel, all other things fell into place. The Rev. W. J. Grier of Belfast, was a special favourite. "Our first word," he writes on one occasion, "was from Mr Grier — a very good word indeed.

He gave a topical address on 'crowns' in the New Testament. I must study this myself some time. The rest of the time was given to prayer. Dear Mr Martin made us feel humble and contrite before God in his evening address. 'The voice of the past to the present' — Ps. 44. It was true to the exegesis of the Psalm and to its outworking in Christian experience. I benefited by this exercise. Dr James du Preez led us in the morning session. I was very much impressed with the message but more particularly with the messenger. Such fragrance I haven't experienced for a long time. This has well nigh disappeared from our devotions. The beauty of the Lord was a reality in every word he uttered and every exercise he engaged in. His subject was 'Salvation — historical preachings'.''

As the older members dropped off from the Conference — especially Dr Lloyd-Jones and Professor John Murray — Mr Morrison's interest in it began to wane. One passage in the diary appears to suggest that a new tendency, which he found objectionable, was beginning to manifest itself among some of the newcomers. This is what he writes: ''I am no lover of intellectual snobbery in any area, especially in the area of theology. I love the theology that I can live on and live for and die for; that was Naboth's creed and culture.''

''It is easy to theorise and speculate in the area of doctrine; it is quite a different matter to translate these verities of the faith into the conflicts and victories of the properly exercised children of God. Every condition has its uses and its blessings for the exercised Christian and as an old writer has said: 'I have found much profit of the heavenly sort in keeping a sorrow-mill wherewith to grind all my suffering into meal for nutrition'.''

Mr Morrison attended the Conference for the last time in 1973.

Shortly before the 1974 Conference he records: ''I wrote yesterday to Mr Iain Murray informing him that I could not be present at the Leicester Conference this year. It has been somewhat unpalatable to me, it has too much emphasis on the intellect — what Hugh Miller would call, logical dogmatics.''

There is a reason to suspect that in his closing years his interest in religious Conferences and Conventions generally had waned. It may be that he had expected too much of them. The idea of evangelical people from different denominations coming together for a few days to discuss matters of common interest in Christian fellowship was an attractive one, but the reality fell short of the expectation. When the days of meeting ended, the participants went their different ways, soon to forget what it was all about. Conventions that made the dispensing of the Lord's Supper a feature of their gatherings were, he believed, carrying their slogan of "all one in Christ Jesus" too far. Whatever suggestion of Christian unity was inherent in the sacrament, primarily, it was a memorial of Christ's death, to be observed "till He come". Admission to the sacrament was to be given by the constituted authorities of the local Church, who had the oversight of the congregation and a special responsibility for their spiritual welfare, which extended to the censure and correction of the erring member, and his restoration on his professing penitence. Discipline, as Mr Morrison so often reminded his people, was regarded by the Reformers as one of the "marks" of the Church, and the Church that lacked this distinction could not rightly claim to be in the Reformed family. Heresy runs amok where discipline is neglected, and the creeds of the Church are evacuated of meaning.

The inter-denominational evangelistic campaigns which have, of recent times, become such a feature of religious life in this country, did not altogether find favour with Mr Morrison. He would allow, indeed, that they provided good opportunities for Christian fellowship, and that the addresses of the invited speakers came under the description of "evangelical" in the present-day usage of the word. But just as the term "Fundamentalism" has become one of the debased words of the modern theological vocabulary, so too has "Evangelicalism". In their endeavour to widen the basis of faith, many Evangelicals have, in the process, weakened it, and have brought about a situation that was envisaged and foretold by Dr Thomas McCrie a century and a half ago.

"A vague and indefinite evangelism," wrote Dr McCrie, "mixed with seriousness into which it is the prevailing disposition of the present age to resolve all Christianity, will, in the natural progress of human sentiment, degenerate into an insubstantial and incoherent pietism, which, after effervescing in enthusiasm, will finally settle into indifference; in which case, the spirit of infidelity and irreligion, which is at present working and spreading to a more alarming extent than many seem to imagine, will achieve an easy conquest over a feeble and exhausted and nerveless adversary."

We have lived to see the outworking of this vague evangelism which lacks the virility that only a definite and Biblical theological basis can impart. Inevitably, this incoherent pietism is accommodating in character. And as the spirit of compromise advances, the spirit of militancy recedes, until we get to the stage that we must not be intolerant of anything. What our fathers roundly called heresy, we must regard as "other aspects of the Truth" which is not seen in its completeness by anybody. Piously sentimental brethren would have us sing with Tennyson:

> "Our little systems have their day,
> They have their day and cease to be;
> They are but broken lights of Thee,
> And Thou, O Lord, art more than they."

How true these words if the "little systems" are indeed ours alone! Our conceptions! Our creations! But if the system be not ours; if it be a Bible-guided formulation of Christian teaching which was no new thing when the Reformers proclaimed it with such amazing effect in the sixteenth century, then it can never "cease to be". It will keep coming back, as repeatedly it has come back, even after ages of spiritual declension, in those seasons of quickening by which it pleases the Lord to build again Sion.

During a fireside conversation in his own Manse Mr

Morrison once expressed his entire agreement with McCrie in the words above-quoted from him. Christian activity in all its branches, he believed, ought to be related to the Church and its historic Creeds as these formulated the eternal verities of the Christian faith. Thus, and thus alone, could the ideal of "all one in Christ Jesus" be attained.

"This new development of late years — holding special services," he writes, "has some latent tendencies, which I am not too happy about. For one thing it tastes of too much of the machine age or in ecclesiastical terminology it tastes too much of priestcraft. What is needed is not more numbers and services but more of the spirit of waiting on God. This new cult is also indicative of a certain void in the life of the Church. And the answer they have provided for this is in the nature of some entertainment. But this is not what is called for."

— 11 —

Mr Morrison, needless to say, rejoiced in the circulation of the Holy Scriptures in the vernacular of the various nations and peoples, and sometimes expressed the wish that more financial support be given to this work and less to the proliferation of modern versions in our own language. It was a good thing, he would argue, that each language-group should have its own standard version, and that the people should become so familiar with its text as to recognise readily the quotations which they heard from it. If the preacher desired to use an alternative rendering of a particular text he was at liberty to do so, and his diligence in this respect might be to the benefit of the hearer. But new translations of the whole Bible tended to confuse the people. He is characteristically blunt in his criticisms.

"Of late," he writes, in December 1978, "I have found some of the versions distasteful to me. For example, I have read through the whole of the American Standard Version during 1978. Even Dr Marshall's New Testament version has disappointed me a few times. Indeed, I have again and again stated that for the last two decades — especially the second of these — nothing has spoiled the 'edge of the sword' and made it less spiritual as much as this irreverent and prayerless handling of the Holy Scripture has done. A little learning is a dangerous thing; and the excessive activity that is current in this area of operation is evidence of such little learning' and the manifestation of its danger.''

Mr Morrison would argue — and not without proof — that new translations of the Holy Scriptures too frequently reflected the vagrant mood of theology in times when the Word of God was treated with less reverence than had been customary in better days. He was by no means an extreme tratitionalist in this respect, and did not claim for the Authorised Version that it was any more than a translation — albeit, the best translation that had appeared in English. But his competent knowledge of Hebrew and Greek qualified him to pronounce on the merits of the different renderings of difficult passages; and there were times when he would indicate his preference for the Gaelic version over that of the Authorised Version itself. But both were the productions of scholarly and devout men who eschewed the evil of ''handling the Word of God deceitfully'', bowed to the authority which it so manifestly claims for itself, and endeavoured with prayerful diligence, to commend it to their readers ''not as the word of men, but as it is in truth, the word of God, which effectually worketh also in you that believe.''

# CHAPTER NINE

# A FAITHFUL WITNESS

**God does not stand for a policy of peace at any price, but of righteousness at any cost.**

—LORAINE BOETTNER.

No one, not even among his sharpest critics, could ever describe James Morrison as a "dumb dog that cannot bark". Indeed, their chief objection was that, in their judgment, he barked too much! To say that sometimes he barked inopportunely might be nearer the mark. Choleric and impatient in temperament, he would never have made a good strategist, and he was constitutionally incapable of the tergiversations of the "wily ecclesiastic". Where his Master's honour was impugned, of His cause at risk, Mr Morrison always felt it his duty to intervene; promptly, and without respect of persons. For instance when a prominent member of the County Council, for whom he had a high regard, one day expressed his irritation by using an unseemly epithet James promptly rounded on him for his lapse. The reproof met with an immediate apology, and the relations between the two men suffered no damage; rather the reverse. The rebuke was recognised as "the smiting of the righteous".

On another occasion he declined an invitation to a dinner that was being laid on in North Uist for a Church of Scotland Moderator because that dignitary had, as Mr Morrison saw it, compromised his Protestantism by attending, in his official capacity, a Roman Catholic service in a Spanish Cathedral. When the two men met at the airport on the morning after the function, Mr Morrison explained that there was nothing personal in his declinature; it was in the nature of a protest against a blatant dalliance, on the part of the Church of Scotland, with the Church of

Rome; an action which would give offence to many in the
Church of Scotland itself.

It did not help any when the Moderator pleaded that his
personal attitude to the Roman Church was not to be judged
by his official action. But the Moderator appreciated the
candour of his new acquaintance, and their subsequent
journey together to Inverness was enjoyed by both and spent
in profitable conversation.

— 2 —

Mr Morrison has sometimes been represented as an over-
rigid denominationalist, and an entirely wrong impression
has been created regarding his relations with ministerial
brethren of other communions. A strong denominationalist
he undoubtedly was, but denominational connection was
not the ultimate consideration in ministerial fellowship.

"I must prove my man — even a minister of the Gospel"
he writes, "before I share my friendship with him. I wish to
co-operate with men in the ministry of the Church of
Scotland that I have found worthy." And he did.

These like-minded brethren co-operated loyally and with
mutual respect in matters of common interest which
affected, or were deemed likely to affect, the welfare of the
community. In the local work of the Lord's Day Observance
Society in particular they stood shoulder to shoulder. Rev.
John Smith of Lochmaddy, Rev. Donald MacRae of
Tarbert and Rev. Angus MacAulay of Uig, in particular,
were all highly-esteemed Church of Scotland colleagues in
the work. Mr Morrison was a Vice-President of the Society
and one of its most active members. A Harrisman himself,
he quotes with approval the strict observance of the Lord's
Day practised by the famous Gaelic poet of Harris, John
Morison — although one doubts that even he would have
followed him in every detail. He writes: "He kept the
Sabbath after the fashion of the Puritans. On that day he
suffered no bread to be cut with a knife; dishes, on one
occasion, washed by a servant contrary to the rules of his
household, he ordered to be put aside and never allowed of
their use for the future. He never retired to bed on Saturday
until the Sabbath broke nor on Sabbath till 12 p.m."

Modern writers on the so-called "Scottish Sabbath" tend to take the line that the strict observance of the day in Scotland was not indigenous to Scotland, but was really an import from Puritan England during the period of coalition between the Scottish Covenanters and the English Puritans when both parties were struggling for very life under the tyranny of the Stuart monarchs, obsessed with their idea of the Divine Right of Kings.

The utter unreliability of this view, however, is clearly shown in the *Cain Domnaig* — the Law of the Lord's Day as observed in the Celtic Church. The *Cain* goes back at least to the beginning of the ninth century, and shows how strictly, in the pre-Roman days, the Celtic Church desired the Lord's Day to be observed. To this end, it lays down Principles; it enumerates Permissions; and it enacts Penalties. And in so doing, it claims to act, not merely by the authority of the Church, but by that of the Son of Man Who Himself is "Lord of the Sabbath".

And it was because James Morrison believed that this Creation ordinance — incorporated in due time in the Decalogue, and observed by our Lord Himself — was binding upon the Church in all ages, that he was such a zealous advocate of its claims. This was the authority with which he opposed Sabbath desecration in all its forms. His diary refers to several of these confrontations.

Attacks on the Lord's Day came from various quarters and under different guises, and they called for constant vigilance. Wherever they appeared Mr Morrison courageously opposed them — not always with success, but with praiseworthy constancy. Of one of these encounters he writes: "On settling down last evening I began reading this manifesto that the Highlands and Islands Development Board prepared on Transport. My heart nearly stopped its beating when they went on to commend 'Sunday Travel', in other words, not a six day week but a seven day week. I prepared a reply for today's meeting. May God use me in this as He used Eleazar of old, when he stood between the living and the dead and the plague was stopped. It was a morning, I sincerely trust, of prayer in the name of the Lord Jesus.''

An entry in 1972 refers to Sunday fishing: "Tonight I asked the Committee to write to the Herring Industry Board and two other similar bodies expressing our serious concern over the appearance of late of fishing boats engaged in fishing on Sabbath nights right along our shores. God spare us this further offence to God's law and to our consciences. He was pleased to encourage me again and again to pray. Dear Uist was near to my heart in it all.''

On another occasion, reference was made at the County Council to the Cairngorms and the training of young people there. "I asked," he writes, "if this meant any interference with the Lord's Day. On my being answered in the affirmative, I made known my complete disapproval.''

He proceeds: "I described the set-up in the Cairngorms as a 'boiling cauldron of offence, and a provocation to Almighty God, which was sure to come under His rebuke in the not too distant future if it was not checked'. I was allowed to make my position clear in this matter but I was not allowed to make a 'motion'. God willing, we shall have to raise this issue in March.''

He was not opposed to the Cairngorms ski-ing facilities as a tourist attraction and local amenity; indeed, a press photograph showed him, with his friend, Rev. Peter Fraser, of Glenmoriston Church of Scotland, trying out the ski-lift for themselves. But he dreaded the Sabbath desecration that he felt sure would result from this form of recreation, and which, indeed, has taken such a heavy toll of life in recent years.

When he met with indifference — and even opposition — in the professing Christian Church to the preservation of the Lord's Day it caused him special grief. This he regarded as the wounding of Christ in the house of His professed friends. South Uist and Barra were strongly Roman Catholic, and their views on Sabbath Observance were certainly not those of the evangelical Protestant community. But even there Mr Morrison had his successes.

I was cheered,'' he writes in one entry, "to see God's

gracious acknowledgment of my witness yesterday. Reference was made to Sabbath work at Barra — work on roads. I challenged this and requested that this should cease forthwith; for that was County Council policy all along. The Committee agreed to request the contractor to refrain from this work on the Lord's Day. I have again and again taken notice of God's interest in me, every time I lifted my voice in defence of His holy Day and Word. This was a day that I relished in every way."

At another time, he speaks of casting himself "in complete prostration at God's blessed footstool" over his "concern that we should get our request through the County Council for a strong representation to the Secretary of State that the weekend fishing in the Minches should be discontinued. The Barra priest could not make it today. We got all we wanted. God ever be praised in thus standing by us and making a way for us against many odds. I endeavoured to praise Him for all this with my whole heart and mind."

— 4 —

Civil Defence presented its own threat. He writes: "I asked an assurance of our Chairman that nothing would be initiated or performed on Sabbath but what was absolutely necessary and urgent. He gave me the unqualified assurance I asked for. Later that day one of the old Councillors said to me: 'I admire you for the way in which you get your word in on behalf of all good causes and I notice that you always get a hearing.' God is my help always. Today the *Press and Journal* referred, very pointedly to my comments yesterday, at the Roads Committee, on Messrs MacBrayne Ltd. and their increase in fares and freights, on all our services."

On another occasion, he writes, "I walked to and from Church today, and spoke to a young man who was closing his shop for the night. I said to him, 'You have reason to praise God now at the end of this day'. He answered: 'I don't understand'. 'Well,' I said, 'see the precious things you have in your shop when many millions at this very hour have nothing.' At once he agreed. Then I added: 'But you fail in one solemn matter. You don't revere the Sabbath.'

He took quite kindly to my words. May God bless them to him. Had I travelled by car to and from Church, God wouldn't have honoured me in that way.''

Wherever the opportunity presented itself to safeguard the sanctity of the Lord's Day, Mr Morrison was quick to seize it. Returning from the General Assembly on one occasion, he writes: ''I was led to cancel my visit to Glasgow in the late evening en route for home. God has so 'covered' me since I left home that I fear lest anything should hurt me in the way. And at worship today I sought His help in my intended visit to the headquarters of the Contractors — Watsons Ltd. — in Corstorphine, Edinburgh. They have charge of the project which the Army have in mind for Benbecula and South Uist. My purpose was to discuss the implications of the Sabbath in this work. It was a very promising contact that I made. They were quite ready to promise me that they would engage in no Sabbath work at all during their time there. May God encourage all this! When our talks were over they sent a car with me to the door of the General Assembly.''

On one occasion, when a Labour Member of Parliament was making a bid to get a Bill through Parliament for the relaxing of the laws relating to Sunday observance, Mr Teddy Taylor, them M.P. for Glasgow Cathcart, made a spirited speech in opposition to the proposed Bill. Mr Morrison was delighted.

It so happened that Mr Taylor was under engagement to address a Free Church Youth conference in Edinburgh around that time, and, on the day appointed for his visit, Mr Morrison phoned me from North Uist to ask if I intended to be at the meeting. On my replying that I did, he charged me to tell Mr Taylor that he had given him a special place in his prayers every day since he (Mr Taylor) had given such a splendid speech for the preservation of the sanctity of the Lord's Day; and that he would continue to do so.

Later in the day I fulfilled my promise to pass on his message. Teddy Taylor looked surprised, and asked who this good man was. I replied that he was a public-spirited minister in a Hebridean congregation whose whole heart was set on the preservation of the spiritual heritage of his country.

Mr Taylor was silent for a moment, and then remarked, "Thank him from me for that message. It has done me good. You have no idea how difficult it is to make a stand on religious and moral questions in the House of Commons. But it will be a strength to me in days to come to know that I have the support of this good man's prayers. I should like to meet him sometime."

At the time, a General Election was in the offing, and the prospect was that a Conservative Government would be returned, in which event Teddy Taylor would be a popular choice for a place in the Cabinet as Secretary of State for Scotland. With this in mind, I replied, "After next election, you probably will meet him. Secretaries of State for Scotland usually make their way up to the Western Isles!"

As it happened, largely as a result of the changing of constituency boundaries, Glasgow Cathcart was captured by Labour at the ensuing election, and when Teddy Taylor, later, returned to the Commons it was as the representative of an English constituency.

James Morrison heard the Election results in 1979 with mixed feelings. "They made me glad, but also sad," he writes. "I was grieved that Mr Teddy Taylor lost his seat. I feel so thankful that Mr Donald Stewart (Scottish Nationalist) continues in his seat. He is next best to the Conservative who had little chance in any case."

Rev. James Morrison and Mr Teddy Taylor never met; but the move to open the flood-gates to Sabbath desecration, to which they were both opposed, was defeated. And who can tell to what extent the defeat was due to the earnest advocacy of the claims of the Lord's Day, by the Christian politician in Parliament, and the fervent prayers of the Highland minister in the seclusion of his study? Are we not assured that "the effectual fervent prayer of a righteous man availeth much"?

After his last visit to Edinburgh, to attend a Lord's Day Observance Society meeting, Mr Morrison enters this comment: "The L.D.O.S. cause has ever been near to my heart and hitherto I have been honoured of Him in having had, again and again, opportunities to serve the interests of the Lords' Day.''

— 5 —

Strangely enough Mr Morrison's abilities as a good Committee man were never fully used by his own denomination. It may be that he was not well enough known throughout the church, or — what is more likely — that his somewhat brusque interventions in Assembly discussions gave the impression to some of his fellow-churchmen that to send him into the Committee Rooms would be like setting a cat among the pigeons! It may not have occurred to them that a flutter in the dove-cots might not be a bad thing! But whatever the cause, the Free Church lost much by her failure to give him a higher place among her counsellors and administrators.

The platform of the General Assembly had little attraction for him, and he seldom occupied it unless he heard something which he judged to be in serious need of rebuke or correction. Sometimes he spoke with a vehemence that spoiled his own case, but he was determined to make his point. He refers to one of these occasions in a late entry in his diary. In a discussion which took rather a theological turn, one or two younger members had spoken of the "image" of God in man in such a way as to suggest that they were not laying as much stress as was proper upon the total depravity of fallen man.

"I was forced to the platform," recalls Mr Morrison: "to rebuke proud flesh on the part of a few who were in danger of neutralising the prayers of the saints for this Assembly. The Lord truly helped me. I referred to the creation of man in God's image and after His likeness. Then it was explained that 'image' had reference to man's Kingship and Lordship over all, and 'likeness' had reference to man's spirituality. By the Fall both were lost without a single qualification. I illustrated this with a reference to Jeroboam who corrupted the worship of ancient Israel, and also Ahab who initiated the worship of corruption in Israel and a cross-section of New Testament times makes this abundantly clear. 'Ye are,' said Christ, 'of your father the devil, and his works ye do.' This was addressed to the most prominent members of the Jewish Church.''

But even when his outspokenness caused irritation, it was soon forgotten, and he was recognised as a loyal son of the Church and a man of prayer. At the devotional exercises of the Assembly he was often called upon to lead the "Fathers and Brethren'' to the throne of grace. He was in a class by himself, and completely unpredictable. Everything was so much part of the man himself, and it was those who knew him best who appreciated him most.

Sometimes his reproofs were tinged with satire, as when he told the congregation — some of whom were surreptitiously removing the wrappers from their favourite confections during worship, ''If you must eat sweets during the service, at least leave the wrappings on when you put them into your mouths. It will be less distracting to those beside you who are trying to concentrate on what is being said.'' In a reference to services which he conducted in Skye on one occasion he writes, ''I expressed my pointed disapproval for the habit of eating sweets in Church. A few afterwards mentioned their agreement with my contention.''

Indeed, those who agreed with Mr Morrison were much more numerous than he knew.

— 6 —

Several years ago, the writer of these lines spent a week in Iona, an island in which I could expect to pass unrecognised. It suited my purpose to remain incognito, for my aim was to give my time to rest and reading. But

> "the best-laid schemes of mice and men
>     gang aft agley."

And mine did!

Within an hour of my arrival I fell in with two ladies who also had arrived that day. They were from North Uist, although one of them had, by that time, lived many years in Glasgow. Inevitably we spoke of St Columba, and of the great debt of the Scottish Church to him and his disciples.

Soon, but not by my initiation, we were discussing the defections of the Church today. The ladies were members of the Church of Scotland, but they were quite frank about certain trends — especially doctrinal — of which they did not approve. In North Uist, they said, the Free Church had a minister whom they admired. He was outspoken, perhaps a bit tactless at times; but he had the courage of his convictions. When they told me that they were referring to Rev. James Morrison of Bayhead, and followed with the question, "Have you heard of him?" I realised that further concealment had become impossible. My disguise was slipping away!

When the embarrassment of the situation was laughingly ended we spoke freely of Mr Morrison, and I was given an enthusiastic description of the work that he was doing for the isle of his adoption. I had the pleasure of visiting the lady from Bayhead in her own home some time thereafter, and of meeting her like-minded husband. It was all the more interesting therefore to find references to them in James's diary. Mr Allan Maclean shared his gardening interest, and that alone would have established a useful point of contact; but quite evidently their conversation rose to higher things.

Here is one of the references.

"Had a conversation with Mr Allan of the Post Office. He referred to the sheep going deeper into the moor with an East wind in their faces. 'They always,' he added, 'graze with their faces in the wind, especially if it is strong.' 'Why is this,' said I. 'The explanation is simple,' said Allan. 'It keeps their coats from being ruffled or untidy in any way, it also after all adds to their comforts. It keeps the cold out better.' This was very suggestive. Must study this further.

"Faith is certainly the better of having the wind in its face. For one thing it stresses the doctrine of 'no confidence in the flesh' in Christian consciousness and experience. It also underlines in our spiritual philosophy of life the paradoxes of faith: 'We glory in tribulations also: knowing that tribulation worketh patience, etc.' A winter's fire burns far more brightly than a summer one does."

The diary contains a reference to the passing of Mrs Maclean.

It runs: "9th June 1977: Last night Mrs MacLean was taken. What pains God takes to teach us that all our well-springs are in Him! I shall miss her help in many ways. She was not of our Church fellowship, but I could depend on her integrity when some of my own fellowship were not so true and loyal."

— 7 —

The passing of Mr MacLean is sorrowfully noted also. "He is much missed," he writes, "for many years it was felt that we could not do without him. He was postmaster here for over fifty years."

His references to the General Assembly are surprisingly few. He was exemplary in his attendance and took an intelligent interest in all its work, especially on the spiritual side of the Church's activities. As a loyal subject of the Crown he seldom missed the courtesy visit of the Lord High Commissioner, for that dignitary was the represenative of the reigning monarch, and James Morrison was no Voluntary in Church Principles. Andrew Melville's definition of Church and State relations held his firm approval. The "twa kingdoms" of Church and State were both under the supreme sovereignty of Jesus Christ, and they were designed to be mutually helpful in their respective functions. The State must not encroach upon the province of the Church, as the Stewart kings were wont to do, and the Church must not usurp the prerogative of the King, as the Church of Rome had been doing.

When the Lord High Commissioner (as notably in the case of that gallant Christian soldier, the late Lord Ballantrae) spoke in terms of personal Christian witness, his visit, understandably, gave special pleasure to Mr Morrison. "Today," he writes on the occasion of Lord Ballantrae's visit, "was a good day with us. The Lord High Commissioner made a very fine impression on us all. The fruit of prayer — the Lord's Presence — was evident in it all. These are moments that God uses to underline for us His pleasure in our way and witness. On the whole, we were conscious of His presiding care and kindness all day and all night.''

The fringe benefits of the General Assembly were, undoubtedly, the opportunities that it offered for the renewal of fellowship with former fellow-students and the friends whose homes had been open to him during his Edinburgh days. He writes, in this connection, ''Set off for the Assembly at 8.20 a.m. This again was a good sederunt. Had dinner with the MacSweens in the Old Mill. Messrs K. J. Nicolson (Barvas), J. Macleod (Shawbost), R. Murray (Skerray), and a Lewis elder were there too. Had tea with the Cunninghams in Caretaker's House at the Church. They are another Scalpay family.''

The Foreign Missions' meeting that evening made a deep impression upon him.

''It was a special evening. Dr Campbell Andrews from Australia was a special treat in his powerful address. The Lord was there. Home at 10.30 p.m.''

But even yet his day was not ended.

''After I finished supper, Rev. Hector Cameron fished me out. We sat in his car *for a long time*.''

''And so,'' as another diarist would have concluded, ''and so to bed.''

But the time of retiral is not disclosed!

# CHAPTER TEN

# THE MINISTER AND HIS BOOKS

"Peace is such a precious jewel that I would give
anything for it but truth".
—MATTHEW HENRY.

Mr Morrison was an avid reader, but was always carefully selective in his choice of books. The range of good literature was so vast, and the time available for reading so limited, that he felt he must always be on his guard against literary trivialities. Above all, he must see to it that even the very choicest of his theological books did not obtrude themselves unduly upon his attention and thereby lessen his time for the study of the source-book of all theology worthy of the name — the Bible. He quotes Dr Andrew Bonar's lamentation, "O my books! How they keep me from *the* Book!"

He, too, feared that distraction, and, in this connection, brings into his diary a reference to a "trackless desert" experience that Dr Campbell Morgan had while he was training to be a teacher.

"For three years he floundered spiritually, reading volumes both attacking and defending the Bible. At last he admitted his total lack of assurance, so he put all his books away in a cupboard, and bought a new Bible.

"I am no longer sure" he said to himself, "that this is what my father claims it to be — the Word of God; but of this I am sure, if it be the Word of God, and I come to it with an unprejudiced and open mind, it will bring assurance to my soul of itself — *and it did.*"

— 1 —

In the development of his theological thinking, James placed himself under the tuition of some of the most eminent divines of the Reformed school, and the Puritans were numerously represented on his shelves. He saw the hand of God in the provision of this great body of Biblical theology at a time when the Church sorely needed instruction in the Faith. These writers had been forced, under pressure of relentless persecution, to make a new appraisal of their faith, and to decide whether it was really worth the sacrifice that its preservation demanded. The result of the re-appraisal was that they became more convinced than ever that the price could never be reckoned too high, even if it meant death itself. The hands of these faithful men dropped myrrh as they wrote, and the fragrance of their devotion still clings to their pages, bringing inspiration and quickening to successive generations of readers. By ejecting them from their pastoral charges their oppressors had provided them with the leisure to write those portly volumes which form the precious legacy of a turbulent age to posterity. Prison itself gave them the quietude — particularly in such cases as John Bunyan and Richard Baxter — to prosecute their holy work. Matthew Henry, who was one of them, spoke for them all when he wrote, "Peace is such a precious jewel that I would give anything for it *but Truth*".

Mr Morrison quotes those words with obvious approval and makes them his own. But even the Truth cannot take possession of the heart unless the Spirit applies it, so our diarist prays, as he takes up his book, in the words of Burrough: "O Lord, open mine eyes and own my heart; Lord, my heart is naturally locked up against Thy Word, so that, except Thou art pleased to put in the key that will fit my heart, it will never open. . . . Let me come with such a praying heart to the Word. Then thou wilt be glorified, and I will be profited."

"How precious it is that one is able to read," he observes on another occassion, "but many read and in the end it were better for them that they had never done so. How essential it is that in this we should set the Lord before us in all things! What are the benefits that we should seek to derive from this exercise? Surely, we should read for the soul's salvation; that is how Christ read in the synagogue, that is how the

Eunuch read in his chariot. And my reading of the word should mean 'I will hear what God the Lord shall speak'."

— 2 —

Mr Morrison's habit of jotting down helpful thoughts that came to him in his studies, and illuminating comments that he found in the course of his reading, has provided us with a choice basket of fragments. Many of these reveal the theological cast of his mind, and the deep penetration of his thought.

We select some of them.

**Imputation of Sin**

Read Matt. 27 — much benefited. Noted that Jesus stood before the Governor — a prisoner at the Bar. When accused by the Chief Priests, etc. He answered nothing and then again when many things were witnessed against Him we read: He answered him (Pilate) never a word. The act of imputation here was most solemn and precious. He is, indeed, preciousness altogether to faith. How our meditations in prayer made this day a blessing to us both!

**The Darkness of Calvary**

I have been led to think of the fearful nature of the period when darkness enveloped the Cross of Christ. What must His soul have suffered during that memorable period! The recent earthquake in Peru was referred to by one of our Missionaries thus: "Standing in the playground I could feel the ground swaying under my feet and I expected it to open at any moment. . . . It seemed to be ages while it lasted, and yet we hear it was just one minute and a half." The concentration of judgment and of the curse that characterised the experience of Christ on the Cross was the equivalent of the saints' merited agonies in hell.

**Divine Sovereignty**

This morning our reading was in John 10: 22-42. The Arminian would have written verse 26 thus: "Ye are not my sheep because ye believe not". Here the Lord says: "Ye

103

H

believe not because ye are not my sheep''. It was my prayer that I should continue in His word in the face of all opposition.

## Jesus' Blood and Righteousness

Were it not for the blood of Jesus Christ His Son I could not hope to escape the damnation of Hell; that is my condition as I stand before God. I rejoiced for a period yesterday that I was conscious of a cleaving to Him; that I had faith to lay hold of His abundant mercy. It is, indeed, my desire that I should know my sinnership so consciously, so realistically that I could always make mention of His righteousness — even His alone; that I would always seek His wisdom, His strength and His ways.

I was much enriched in a reflection on Lev. 4: 17, 18. Here we have the blood . . . before the Lord . . . before the veil; the blood upon the horns of the altar . . . the blood at the bottom of the altar. It was here foundational to the altar.

A worthy man in Stoer, Duncan Kerr, once made this statement in prayer *"Lord, it is not thy righteousness alone we desire, but thyself"*. When we questioned the dear man on this he said "many people even in Stoer, would like to have this righteousness to cover them from wrath in the great day, but nothing else. On the other hand I trust my whole-hearted concern is to have the Lord Himself to clothe me, to feed me, to be my all and in all, my wisdom, righteousness, sanctification and redemption. Even when the Christian is in love with heaven it is for the Lord's sake. Praise is there and as he wishes to praise God he longs for the place in the interest of the praise. Same applies to the holiness of heaven. He thirsts for heaven in order to please God perfectly.''

## The Son of Man

How precious it is that the Saviour is both Son of God and Son of Man! As Man every member of His body and every faculty of His soul suffered because the sin he atoned for reigned in our flesh and spirit. The scene of defeat became the scene of a glorious victory.

### Speaking the Truth in Love

I prayed that the fire should ever burn on the altar at which I served; that He should ever answer me by fire. I also endeavoured to pray at worship that I should do all this in love after His example in the words read. It is only His sweet anointing that will enable me to speak the truth in love. *And sometimes it is easier just to speak the truth than it is to speak it in love.*

### The Mysteries of Providence

I read a few chapters in Cooper's book on Skye. It renewed my interest in the depth of the Divine Sovereignty. Surely it will take eternity itself to unravel the mysteries that attended the Highland clearances of those days. Men and women who were, indeed, the salt of the earth suffered physical and mental and spiritual torments beyond our computation. But these experiences of life and of death, and the thought of eternity entered into the warp and woof of the character, piety and high idealism of the Western nation that emerged from it all. Just as the Cross of Christ in the objective sense was foundational to all life and blessing that followed so the Cross of Christ in this subjective sense gave birth to all this again in Christian experience.

### What God can Do

I have had a petition given me of late that has fitted in well with our emphasis over the years on the Sovereignty of God. It is this: "Show us what thou canst do" and He has done so again and again, in the numbers attending and in the individuals attending. I saw one person present last night and again today that I have seldom seen in Church on any weekday. When I intimated the Communion on the Sabbath before the Communion I said that I wasn't going to say anything but just one word and leave all to Him. The Word was "Think of this time as one of giving more than getting", and I explained that that was not in terms of money, though there was a place for that too — it was a giving of self to God in obedience, in reverence and in honour.

### The Manifestation of Christ's Glory

Before the prayer-meeting tonight I recalled a question that the late Angus MacAulay once put to me regarding the healing of the youth out of whom Jesus cast an evil spirit. "What do you make of the statement that as he was yet a coming, the devil threw him down and tare him?" (Luke 9: 42).

I could not be quite sure of the right answer. Angus himself maintained that it was Christ's way of showing forth His glory to allow the worst to happen before intervening, so that His conquest might appear all the more wonderful. Tonight I understood this better than at the time he raised the question, and it helped me.

### The Domination of Love

I have received the *Expository Times* for this year. In this issue the material is in the main somewhat shadowy, abstract and abstruse; indeed much ado about nothing — a kind of scholarly *pot-pourri*. But one sentence I read did me good: "There is one thing, and one thing only, that keeps fear within its proper bounds, and that is the experience of love. Where love is freely given and received fear ceases to dominate." Perfect love casteth out fear (1 John 4: 18).

### All in the Covenant

I continued my reading in *The Preachers of Scotland* by W. G. Blaikie. Regarding William Guthrie of Fenwick, neither his love of humour, nor of sport seems to have interfered with his heavenly-mindedness; for even amid the glee and hilarity of a fishing party he would invite his companions to some secluded spot that they might join in pouring out their hearts to God. With reference to Guthrie's book, *The Christian's Great Interest,* John Owen said "that little book is my *vade mecum* and there is more theology in it than in all the folios I have written". He, Mr Guthrie, was ever insistent that God had put "all the mercies of His people both temporal and spiritual mercies, all enduements, yea all things, not excepting the shoes that you wear on your feet — all are put in the charter of the covenant". Would that I were so taught and blessed in terms of the covenant and its charter. The Lord be pleased to endue me with this power all my days.

## Serving the Lord

The story is told of an old shoemaker, that he once wanted to become a minister, but the way had never opened up. He was the friend of a young divinity student and when this student was commissioned to preach the gospel the old shoemaker asked for the favour of being allowed to provide his shoes for him, so that the shoemaker could feel that the preacher was wearing his shoes in the pulpit for which he never qualified himself.

## Christ is All

"Christ for us, our atoning sacrifice, Christ upon us, our robe of righteousness, Christ over us, our blessed master, Christ underneath us, our sure foundation, Christ in us, our living power, Christ beside us, our perfect example, Christ around us, our wall of fire, Christ before us, our everlasting heritage" (*Christian,* 31st January 1964).

## Sleeping Disciples

Monday meeting was truly sweet. Angus said in his prayer, with reference to the disciples sleeping in the ship on the sea of Galilee, "Christ slept just as they slept, but they couldn't sleep as He slept". That was very shrewd. I had read Mk. 4: 35-41 before he prayed. And there reference is made to Christ's sleep. I touched on this, too.

## "Faithful in Business"

One of the things that has seriously damaged the Cause of Christ in our time is sheer laziness. Worldly men who at the same time are energetic and progressive in their chosen careers and professions are simply nauseated with ministers of religion who lounge around fawning on this party and then on another with nothing nobler in view than their own comforts and final retirement. We should, as ministers of the gospel, be at least as conscientious in our calling as the boxer or runner or climber or fisherman is in his area of interest. Indeed, I verily believe that the very tragedy that has overtaken the life of this nation industrially is in great measure the result of this grave dereliction of duty within the precincts of the professing Christian Church itself.

## Ritual and Formality

I took to my study today, and closely studied Hosea 7: 1-9. I didn't cover all that area, but it was a study that made me whole; that is always a quality of the peace of God. I made a particular point with the ''cake not turned''. Here was an emphasis on ritual without experience — something akin to the Roman Catholic delusion; where the Priest does it all at the moment. We ourselves are of the same pattern; when we enter the House of God; hear the reading; take part in the singing; rise to the prayer; listen to the preaching; join again in the singing; rise to the Benediction and then walk out, without any realisation of what it all really and savingly meant. The ritualist can be very punctilious also with, at the same time, no knowledge or love present in any single exercise of it.

He hits off the ''delusion'' of the Mass by quoting a story that appeared in *The Bulwark* in 1965.

''An elderly Catholic woman crossed and re-crossed the Channel many times, always clutching her bottle of 'holy water', always securing kindly fiscal immunity. Eventually, however, one horrid Customs man took the bottle, pulled the cork out and declared sternly — 'That, Madam is whisky'. Whereupon she promptly exclaimed 'Glory be to God! A miracle!' Roman Catholics are asked, nay compelled, to accept a vastly less credible 'miracle' every time they receive Mass''. The doctrine of the transubstantiation of the water into the actual body and blood of Christ in the Mass is indeed ''a blasphemous fable and a dangerous deceit'', as the English Reformers described it.

Worship had a breath of repentance for me this morning. Our late dear Principal John MacLeod used to say that Godly sorrow and Repentance were two of the believer's best friends throughout life. So much so that at death the saint might say: "Now we do part, but you have been so infinitely precious to me that even at heaven's gate I am loth to part from you".

## Reasons for going to Church

I read this in a book that came to my hand last night: "I have in my congregation a worthy aged woman, who has for many years been so deaf as not to hear the loudest sound and yet she is always one of the first in the meeting. On being asked the reason for her constant attendance . . . she answered: 'Though I cannot hear you I come to God's house because I love it and desire to be found in His ways: and He gives me many a sweet thought upon the text when it is pointed out to me. Another reason is that I am in the best company . . . the honourable of the earth. I am not satisfied with serving God in private; it is my duty and privilege to honour Him regularly and constantly in public.'"

## An Acceptable Offering

I was touched keenly with this word in "Luther's *anecdotes*". Luther once visited a dying student. The good professor asked the young man what he should take to God, in Whose presence he was shortly to appear. The young man replied "everything that is good, everything that is good". Luther, surprised, said, "But how can you bring Him everything that is good seeing you are but a poor sinner?" The pious youth said, "I will take to my God in heaven, a penitent humble heart sprinkled with the blood of Christ." "Truly," said Luther, "this is everything good; then go, my son; you will be a welcome guest to God."

## The Use and Limitation of the Law

The Ten Commandments are like a mirror. "You look in a mirror to see if your face is dirty, but you don't take the mirror to wash your face."

## The Word and Prayer

Impressed much with these words from Dr D. M. Macintyre and quoted in *The Evangelical Presbyterian:*

"One who has prayed the Bible through, turning the Word of God into supplication, is far advanced in holiness". He has taught me a little of this. Sometimes my texts on Sabbath have been praying matter for me before, but especially after, they were preached from. I am still at school in this, as in many other matters.

## The Reward of Obedience

John 21: 6. *"Cast the net on the right side of the ship."*
Strange that they so readily complied with His instruction. They had caught nothing. They were experienced fishermen. Humanly speaking it was out of season to cast the net now. And who might this stranger be in any case? What right had he to request this? But the word of the one on the shore was the word of a King — *the* King. And where the word of a King is there is power. This is the word that called Abraham from his country and his idolatry.

## A Prophetic Action

Worship last night was a special exercise. I was asked to take the opening prayer, and all of a sudden I was led to pray for Mary's love and loyalty when she anointed the Lord Jesus and the house was filled with the odour of the ointment. How this action must have entered into a vision, on the part of the Beloved, of the crown of thorns being transformed into the crown of purest gold — of glory; of a sin-cursed experience to be exchanged for the prophetic anointing with the oil of joy above His fellows — His companions!

## Law and Grace

It is not easy at all times to realise the difference between our knowing ourselves under the Law and not under Grace. The confessions of Pharaoh: "I have sinned . . . The Lord is righteous, and I and my people are wicked . . . intreat the Lord for it is enough . . . I have sinned against the Lord your God and against you . . . forgive my sin" — Exod. 9: 27, 28; 10: 16, 17. These and other such words in the Scriptures are the confessions of men under the Law and not under Grace. What then is the difference between such confessions and those that are made by such as are under Grace? The Rod — the Word of the Lord — that the wicked experiences in such areas of life is the same as the righteous has experience of; and while under chastisement for his sins the saint of God, particularly in the first stages of his trial, finds it hard to discern any difference. In his case, however, this is not an end in itself; this is unto salvation. Again the difference is that he has a place in the Lord's intercession.

**Self-Abasement**

Surely, surely I should be in the dust before Him when the seraphims, whose faces and feet have never been soiled, veil or "cover" their faces and feet before Him. I never come into His house or even before Him without a desire to know myself as a sinner in His Presence. Yes, I am conscious of the danger of seeking to know *the comforts of faith* without the *disciplines of repentance.* I fear this spirit in the Church more than I fear atheism in the world.

— 3 —

As the years went by Mr Morrison's bond with North Uist increased in strength until it gained the mastery, even over Scalpay; but nostalgic thoughts of his Harris home were never far away. A diary-entry during his Manse restoration activities in North Uist reveals the sentimental cast of his mind.

"The joiners were here and when they had to do business in painting and papering preparations I considered it fair to them and to the Manse's interests to 'abide by the stuff'. I have much experience in this whole field. I had two experiences that deeply moved me. In preparing some paint we were anxious to have a little blue for a very particular reason. This blue paint turned up in a small tin that had been in a corner for well over 30 years. The name on the tin 'Peacock — Buchan' was what moved me. This was the order of the day in my young days for all the fishing boats at dear old Scalpay. And the contents of the tin were as fresh as the day they were put there. I feel happy that this colour now graces an area of the Manse — the scullery.''

James would never choose change just for the sake of changing, and even when the change was obviously for the benefit of the people involved he tended to look back longingly to the old order. He welcomed the introduction of electric power to his Manse, but fond thoughts of the old way of things still lingered, He writes: ''The electric power was in use in the Manse last night for the first time. That affected us both very much. The oil lamps were now to be laid aside — possibly for ever. There was something responsive about them; one could trim them and they seemed to respond in turn. This new power is so aloof, so impersonal; there is hardly any feeling of kinship with us. The old lamps were the accompaniments of the past; they were part of the life of our worthy fathers. They betokened a lower existence, in terms of human or modern values, than obtains with us at the ordinary or mundane levels of life.''

Sentimental? But aren't we all? Or nearly all? Those of us who sampled life in the Highlands 60 or 70 years ago will easily be drawn into this nostalgic mood. For we too have sat in the ingle-neuk beside a glowing peat fire, with a parafin lamp beside us, yielding us warmth as well as light as we revelled in a favourite book. And those of us who sat in the old Free Church of Scalpay will remember the cluster of tilley lamps which radiated warmth as well as light on a cold night; at the same time, by their subdued hissing, hushing us, as it seemed, into a reverent silence and expectancy such as became the House of God.

Ah well, it seems to be the rule of progress that there cannot be gain without counter-balancing loss.

But memories remain.

# CHAPTER ELEVEN

## THE STUDENT OF THE WORD

**The Resurrection was the Father's kiss of acceptance
of the whole work of the Atonement.**

—JAMES MORRISON.

James Morrison entered the Gospel ministry in obedience to a call that, to him, was clear and compelling. In a diary entry dated 17th May, he reiterates that fact. He writes: "Dr Alexander Carlyle of Inveresk declared that he entered the ministry to please others. It is said that when he preached his first sermon he was inwardly pleased that he had chosen the ministry, because a young lady told him that she was charmed with his oratory. He gloried in the fact, according to his own reckoning, that he had delivered the Church of Scotland from fanaticism. He prided himself also that he vindicated the right of ministers to go to the theatre. Well, that type of motivation has had nothing to do with my choice of preaching the Gospel of the grace of God. One aspect of this that has played its part in my life all along is a passion to overturn anything or everything that is not consistent with the mind of Christ."

— 1 —

It is a matter for regret that Mr Morrison's yield in written sermons is meagre almost to the point of non-existence. He was not a man to submit himself to the discipline of the pen, and the "paper-minister" as he called him, was not his model. That does not mean, however, that he was slip-shod in his preparation for the pulpit; far otherwise. Like King David, he would not offer unto the Lord that which had cost him nothing. As his diary reveals, he spent long and busy hours in study and prayer, and he was his own sternest critic. But the quality of his sermons could depend very much on the mood of the moment. He was easily put off, and an untoward incident could have the effect of changing a good sermon into a tirade. Nobody was more aware of this than himself. Time and again he takes himself to task in his diary. The following entry is typical: "How I should mourn for my petulance, my excitability, my churlishness! The Lord grant me to nail this, and without delay."

Dr D. M. MacIntyre tells of one of the Scots lords, in the days of the Covenant, who, one day, sat listening to Samuel Rutherford as he stormed against the prevailing decisions of the time. The nobleman could not go the whole way with the preacher; but when Rutherford turned from his polemics to speak of "the fragrance of Sharon's fair and bleeding Rose" the restless hearer came under the spell of the Cross. "Ay," he was heard to ejaculate, "haud you there! Now you are right!"

There were some of the good people of North Uist, we believe, who felt the same about their minister. They might part company with him in some of his views on current happenings, but when he brought them to the Cross they were with him. Ejaculations would be disfavoured in the Free Church of North Uist, but in the silent sanctuary of the heart there was a whisper that somehow reached the pulpit: "Ay, haud you there!" And their prayers helped to bring him a fuller vision of the glory of Calvary which the Holy Spirit enabled him to share with his hearers.

— 2 —

Sometimes, in his diary, he gives us his text, and the divisions of his discourse, and we are thus enabled to share in the feast of fat things which he has prepared. Here is a sample. The text is John 19: 12-13. *"Then the band and the captain and officers of the Jews, took Jesus, and bound Him, and led Him away . . ."* And the heads are:

1. Jesus bound — by whom?
2. Jesus bound — when?
3. Jesus bound — why?
4. Jesus suffering — to what purpose?

Find the answer to these questions and you find the very heart of God. He introduces us again to his study on another Saturday evening with the following report of his preparatory work: "Since the morning He seemed to spare me a look of approval, at least my soul was conscious of His inspiration in prayer and I benefited as a result of this in my studies. I studied for the noon service. Lk. 11: 49. *'Wist ye not that I must be about my father's business.'* (1) Christ's mediatorship is in view here; (2) the *content* of this 'business'; (3) the Son's 'must' in its accomplishment. The Father is *satisfied* in this 'business'; the Son is *satisfied;* the Spirit of God is *satisfied;* all the perfections of the Godhead are satisfied and honoured here. This benefits all the seed of Abel; all the seed of the promise. I prepared Jude 24, 25 for the evening service. God be over all; in all; for all; with and through all."

Family worship often suggested themes for the pulpit. For example — 3rd December 1971: "I was led at morning worship to arrange my thoughts around Isa. 6: 1-7, the death of King Uzziah. What a holy meditation I had here! It made the day so pleasant for me from beginning to end! Surely God is for me and with me notwithstanding the tunnel I had to pass through on Thursday and Friday. I have often noticed how easy it is to prepare a sermon when one is led of Him. And He has again and again come to my rescue when I was thus pressed for time, as I was on this occasion. My thoughts were arranged under three major headings: (1) the vision of God; (2) the confession evoked; (3) the forgiveness realised. I took note of the framework of providence here. Death is noted; a king's death. It might even be possible to recount the nature of the king's death. Leprosy had entered into Uzziah's experience — like the old progenitor — Adam. But that only made the vision of the Lord Jesus Christ all the more pertinent and precious."

On 1st February 1970 he preached on Acts 3:16. *"What shall we do to these men?"*, and the points considered were:

1. *The Miracle* — the healing of the impotent man.

2. *The Message* which it conveyed — see Peter's address, vv. 8-14.
3. *The Question* to which it gave rise — v. 16.

Again, the groundwork of a good Bible meditation.

On a Saturday evening in December 1971 he discloses his plans for the morrow.

"For the evening service I had under consideration 1 Cor. 15: 51, 52: *Behold, I show you a mystery, we shall not all sleep, but we shall all be changed. . . .*

1. The *Mystery;* the *'change'.*
2. The *'some'* who will sleep.
3. The *'some'* who will not sleep.
4. The *'all'* who will be changed.

And what a change it will be! No change has ever been effected in time like this change. This will be a short work — 'in a moment' . . . in a glance of an eye — like an arrow from a bow, like a flame of fire or a rushing wind. God has been active thus in life but few took note; when Noah entered the Ark the flood came; so with Sodom and Gomorrah; so at the Red Sea; so in all areas of providence and redemption. But this Day all will witness and experience this change. My soul wait thou on God; my soul hope thou in His mercy; my soul rejoice thou in the Lord. God made me to end this day somewhat in peace as far as my preparation for the pulpit was concerned."

— 3 —

The following are additional specimens of his sermon-outlines as given in his diary:

"Zech. 13: 7, and the latter part of it: *Smite the Shepherd, and the sheep shall be scattered; and I will turn my hand upon the little ones.* The Shepherd. Jacob's reference to this relationship is very significant. God *fed* him all his life long. He was his Shepherd, and this implied God's care of his spirituals as well as his temporals; so it was in the case of Israel when David was God's shepherd. The Lord said: 'Thou shalt feed my people Israel and thou shalt be a Captain over them, over Israel'. And this rises to its height in the Lord Himself, for He was the good Shepherd, the great Shepherd, the chief Shepherd. And how sweetly this is committed to the Apostles in the final form of their commission: (1) *The Smitten Shepherd;* (2) *The Scattered Flock;* (3) *The Resurrection blessing. I will turn my hand upon the little ones* — gathering them together again.''

\* \* \* \*

"Heb 5: 9. *And being made perfect, he became the author of eternal salvation.* . . . The Son of Man perfected here. This was in a certain place and at a certain time. This has reference to His death and burial. And the perfection denotes:

1. *The sinlessness of the Lord Jesus.* He was holy, harmless, undefiled separate from sinners. When the first Adam failed the last Adam stood the test right through.

2. *The completion of the work of atonement.* He not only fulfilled all that was written in the Law, the Prophets and the Psalms, but He also finished the work the Father gave Him to do. He drank the whole cup which was allocated to Him.

3. *That He was perfected. In the most positive* sense His *soul* was set free, His *body* was set free. He was now qualified to assume all His mediatorial offices."

\* \* \* \*

"Luke 23: 34: *Father, forgive them; for they know not what they do.*

1. The *Deed* referred to.
2. The *Plea* offered 'they know not. . . .'
3. The *Blessing* sought for them.
4. The *Relationship* in which He sought it. 'Father.'

First word when He was crucified was 'forgive'. Prayed for the souls of His murderers. As soon as His blood began to be poured out the Great High Priest began to intercede. His ministry here is being closely knit to His death. God's power was manifested in and through the shed blood. This is the place for repentance and faith."

\* \* \* \*

117

*"(I) was before a blasphemer and a persecutor, and injurious; but I obtained mercy, because I did it ignorantly in unbelief.* 1 Tim. 1: 13. (1) *The life he lived in the flesh —* blasphemy, persecution and arrogancy characterised it all; (2) *But he obtained mercy;* (3) Why? It was all done in ignorance and unbelief. Here ignorance and unbelief are in close connection. Where ignorance holds sway unbelief reigns also. Mr Alexander of Liverpool made a statement in our pulpit when he was here a few years ago that continued with me: "Of all the evils that have plagued us of late years, nothing has been more threatening than the unbelief, the positive heathenism that has entered our homes and our lives in temporals and spirituals everywhere".

*    *    *    *

*"Blessed is he whose transgression is forgiven. . . .* Psalm 32: 1-2; (1) The *Condition Described;* (2) The *Blessing Experienced;* (3) *The Blessing Acknowledged.* Referred in this sermon to purity of worship in both English and Scottish Churches between 1661 and 1688; how this continued in Scotland after 1707 and up to 1860. What has befallen us now when the Church of Scotland is anxious to change her hymnary and even introduce pop music into her worship. And this obtains in nearly all the Scottish Churches now. When Israel assembled at the foot of Sinai the greatest wonder of all that characterised its fellowship was that God declared He was to dwell in their midst. And as a token of this favour He supplied the pattern of His own tabernacle and the worship connected therewith, commanding them to do all things according to the pattern showed them in the mount."

*    *    *    *

"Text: 1 Cor. 12: 6: *diversities of operations . . . but the same God.* It is obvious that the Apostle here is under great pressure. The mercenary spirit in Corinth which in its primitive and pagan form made for fierce rivalries and passionate personal ambitions could still exercise its influence within the area of the Church at Corinth. But the

118

Apostle was encouraged to think that they would add to their enrichment in Christ 'all utterance and knowledge', and the highest and best of all — *love*. So in this chapter he relates the diversities of gifts to the same Spirit; the differences of ministries to the same Lord; the diversities of operations to the same God. But in so doing, and with his commendation, he at the same time is anxious to point out a 'more excellent way'. Nothing can be substituted for love. That is part of *our* weakness too. Making money and hoarding it in the capacity of petty merchants has been our bane for too long. God grant us the spirit that developed here in terms of the two epistles to the Corinthians.''

\*   \*   \*   \*

(Outline of sermon preached at the introduction of his cousin, Rev. John Morrison, B.A., to Fort William):
"Acts 9: 13, 17; 13: 2:

1. Saul of Tarsus — the *Sinner* (v. 13:)
2. Saul of Tarsus — the *Brother* (v. 17:)
3. Saul of Tarsus — the *Apostle* (13: 2)

The means employed in the Transformation.''

\*   \*   \*   \*

"I wakened to a good day — sunny and calm, though quite cold. Worship was fragrant and full of power this morning. Text: Jude 1: 1 — 'called': (1) *the common call; the effectual call; (2) the author of this call; (3) the end product of this call; (4) the call and the atonement; (5) the finality of this call.* The atmosphere of the Church today was very congenial to preaching.''

\*   \*   \*   \*

"*But when the fulness of the time was come, God sent forth His Son, made of a woman, made under the law, to redeem them that were under the law that we might receive the adoption of sons.* Gal. 4: 4-5. I tried to confine myself to three reflections on this word. *(1) The fulness of the time; (2) The Redemption Effected; (3) The Purpose of the Redemption.* The Adoption of Sons. God never works

119

I

untimeously. The matter is important but the method is always worthy of it. So here everything is laid under tribute to answer His purposes, to effect His ends. I often think of the whole Old Testament economy in terms of a woman with child; and the New Testament as the time in which we have the birth of this Son of Promise.''

\* \* \* \*

"Took note at worship today of 2 Sam. 18: 28: *All is well;* then of verse 21: *Go tell the King what thou hast seen.* It is interesting and instructive to compare 'the men' in this verse and the 'sons of men' in Ps. 4: 2. The big men in the latter are the same as the small men in the former word. It is just parabolic of what enters into the sanctification of the believer. He begins 'big' and ends 'small'. It was also true that when these in Ps. 4: 2 were sons of men — men of importance — not ordinary men in the crowd — David's lot and portion appeared to be very unprosperous and umpromising. When the change was effected in their condition — when they became frail men — it was then, too, that David came into his own again — to his throne and into God's Sanctuary. Dying and living, suffering and reigning with Him are never to be separated here — while sin remains.''

\* \* \* \*

"Text: Hebs 4: 16: *Let us therefore come boldly to the throne of grace, that we may obtain mercy, and find grace to help in time of need.*

1. Where do we come? *The Throne of Grace.*
2. *Why do we come!* Because mercy and grace are to be found there.
3. *The Help is seasonable.* In Time of Need.
4. *How do we come?* Let us come boldly . . . that is in the full assurance of faith.''

\* \* \* \*

"Text: Rom. 5: 20: *Moreover, the law entered, that the offence might abound. But where sin abounded, grace did much more abound.* I never could see so clearly the definition of law as I did today. It appeared in terms of: first the blade; then the corn and finally the full corn in the ear. The law in seed-form finding expression in the blade was the moral law; the second stage, the ceremonial law; while the full corn was the New Testament as it found expression in the fulfilment of all that preceded it. It was a very searching and soul-enriching word to me. The service did me much good."

*     *     *     *

"John 16: 23: *In My Name.* I had much liberty in Sollas particularly on the aspect of Christ's name in its relation to prayer. I referred to Noah's sacrifice after the Flood as the initiation of God's covenant of peace inasmuch that He said 'I will not again curse the earth for man's sake' and this was in virtue of a greater sacrifice which Noah's sacrifice prefigured. In referring to the Saviour's obedience and atonement I was led to think that it evermore filled God's nostrils with the fragrance of it, that it involved the eternal acceptance of all for whom He died and was buried. 'Their sins and iniquities I will remember no more' for this was substituted for them.

*     *     *     *

"Text: 1 Sam. 7: 12: *Ebenezer.* Touched on *(1) hitherto* as descriptive of time and place — God has a perfect wholeness in all His works. I referred to Samuel's circuit — Bethel, Gilgal and Mizpeh here. There were Ebenezers all along that pathway — Bethel, Gilgal, Mizpeh. And this is true in particular when we turn to the New Testament to Bethlehem; Nazareth; Gethsemane and Calvary. Surely 1560 — the first Assembly of the Church of Scotland — was another such; and 1843 and 1900 also. And there are Ebenezers in our own lives. The time of love in conversion is one; many providences in the way could so be called; many deliverances in temptation could be so described; many divine acknowledgments in the path of duty could be included. (2) The helper: *the Lord.* (3) The helped; Us — though so unworthy.''

\*　　\*　　\*　　\*

"God was my help today. I began my studies early. He called me to pray again and again. I spent the whole day on Deut. 8: 2-3: *thou shalt remember. . . .* Studied it fairly closely. These words entered my mind more than once of late months. But this became more emphatic around Wednesday. I saw the words quoted in a small book. It was an encouragement to me — this preparation — throughout the whole day. When I finished I began reading in Vol. V of Jonathan Edwards' works. Touched much with the following words: 'Sin casts contempt upon the authority and law of God; but this by the contrivance of our redemption is made an occasion of the greatest honour done to that same authority and to that very law. It was a greater honour to God's authority that Christ showed such great respect and such entire subjection to it, than the perfect obedience of all the angels in heaven. Man by his sin showed his enmity against the holiness of God. But this is made an occasion of the greatest manifestation of God's holiness. *The holiness of God never appeared to so great a degree as when God executed vengeance upon His own dear Son.*''

\*　　\*　　\*　　\*

"I was interested in John 21: 1-10 — for the prayer meeting. This was the third time He made Himself known to His disciples after He had risen from the dead. He had showed them His hands and His side, according to John; His hands and His feet, according to Luke. Noted that they remained in Jerusalem for that week. Poor Thomas was none the worse for that. How considerate the Blessed One is! He doesn't leave a single sheep behind. And how gracious on His part that Galilee was to be the place of meeting! Jerusalem might suit for His Crucifixion but Galilee must be the place of fellowship after His resurrection. To the poor the Gospel is preached. The disciples led by Peter went fishing. There is no word of rebuke in the narrative in relation to this. There were only seven disciples present; perhaps the rest had not arrived. Peter was not the man to be idle. Why should they go hungry when they could fish and had nets and boats? There might have been, at the same time, a little impatience on their part."

\*     \*     \*     \*

"I took the monthly meeting in Glendale. Text: Heb. 6: 11. *And we desire that every one of you do show the same diligence to the full assurance of hope to the end.* It was the sweetest service of all. I just felt that God was at work in that little company. I quoted a word from Bishop Moule's letters that God accompanied with power. He was replying to a friend's letter. In that letter the friend referred to the Bishop's late wife. In his letter the Bishop described her passing — just a year to the day before — and still an open wound; but he added *no part of it is allowed to turn septic.* The person of the Lord Jesus Christ is the balm that is applied to it all. In quoting this I emphasised that in our language this meant the eternity and divinity of His person — the Lord, the Saviourhood — Jesus; the Lordship and Kingship over His Church for ever — the Christ. And what balm that is! May He ever apply it to all our needs!"

\*     \*     \*     \*

"We read Mk. 15: 47. Text: *And Mary Magdalene and Mary the mother of Jesus beheld where He was laid.* We wondered where the disciples were. But we noted that God is never without His man, and right nobly did Joseph of Arimathea do his work. Pilate marvelled if He were already dead. But God again never fails to honour His word. Possibly the Beloved was the first of the three to die, because His was the greatest sorrow of all. What a scene is presented to us here! The Lord of life sharing in this experience of death and the grave; it is more: it is the beginning of the end of death and the grave. My soul, enter thou into this joy of the Lord."

\*     \*     \*     \*

"Gen. 32: 1-2: Two Hosts. (1) *Definition of Mahanaim;* (2) *Ministry of God and Angels here;* (3) *The Rebuke to our carnality*. This holy and heartening experience rendered Jacob's immediate past meaningful and profitable; while it was at the same time preparatory for further dangers that lay ahead. What a complex case of need Jacob had! Even on the purely human plane his was no ordinary trial — mothers and families; servants and maid servants and much cattle, were all his responsibility. and yet the concerns of the soul took precedence of all. Just as the entrance and appearance of Esau was the embodiment and personification of all evil on the human plane so it was also and in a more special sense on the plane of the spiritual and in relation to the souls concerned here. But Esau and his host were more than matched by God's host.''

\*　　\*　　\*　　\*

"Judges 7: 5-7: *The Test at the Waters*. I made it clear that the distinction lay between those who kneeled down and those who did not; those who lapped — as a dog does — and those who drank. Gideon, the General — and all he stood for — the cause of God in Israel — took precedence of all other things in the case of the 300 who lapped; while the flesh, and all it represented, governed the thinking of the rest. But I emphasised, too, that the 300 had need of the water just like the rest. And in the spiritual warfare God has honoured us in giving us an opportunity to give even a cup of cold water to His worthy people.''

\*　　\*　　\*　　\*

**The Priesthood of Christ**

Thornwell: "The New Testament gives a prominence to the priesthood which it nowhere concedes to the kingly or prophetic offices of Christ. It was the very end of His incarnation that He might be a merciful and faithful High Priest''.

"Text: Matthew 26: 6-10: The Anointing in Bethany. I had much liberty in delivering this message and I was convinced of its timeliness. With this 'smash and grab' philosophy of the hour, and Christians involved in it, this word was helpful to us all. Solemn and fearful to think that even the Apostles were ensnared and corrupted with Judas's lust for money. He made them indignant with Mary's good work. Made them to refer to this holy and happy experience of the Saviour at Mary's hands as 'waste' — *apoleia* — destruction. What 'casting down' will be effected at death! Surely man walketh in a vain show!"

\* \* \* \*

## No other gods before Me

"How we need to discipline our hearts in terms of the first commandment! Monotheism may be our glib confession; while polytheism may be our prevailing practice. The Greeks of old were wont to quote the legend of the youth Narcissus, who came to be obsessed with his own image reflected in a well, as an illustration of this pernicious cult of self-praise, of self-seeking and self-sufficiency. At the same time it was my plea that the fear of Isaac should fall on all my associates and that this should be so all day. The Lord was pleased to hear me."

\* \* \* \*

## Help from Thomas Adams

"I took to some reading for most of the day. I felt weak and helpless in the hands of a tempting demon; that is the only way in which I could describe the nature of my buffetings. After I continued with my reading for a period I seemed to keep on a more steady course in the path of obedience. I had my reading in a sermon by Mr Thomas Adams, the Puritan. Text: Ecc. 9: 3: *'The heart of the sons of men is full of evil, and madness is in their heart while they live: and after that they go to the dead'*. Adams writes: 'Virtues are not given by birth nor doth grace follow generation by regeneration' (p. 255). The good heart is a receptacle for the whole Trinity; and therefore it hath three angles as if the three Persons of that one Deity would inhabit there. The Father made it; the Son bought it; the Holy Ghost sanctifies it; therefore all three claim a right in the heart."

\* \* \* \*

## The Refuge of the Altar

"The four corners of the altar in appearance would resemble horns — 1 Kings 11: 28; Ps. 118: 27. To these the victims would be bound. Criminals — like Joab and Adonijah — caught hold of them; but these horns could not protect a heinous criminal. But, as Mather says, 'He that flies to Christ, and hangs upon Him, whose power was typified by these horns, shall never be plucked thence'."

\* \* \* \*

## Heirs of God (Rom. 8: 17)

"We are put into God's will — joint-heirs with Christ; but we are not joint-purchasers. He purchased all. He paid at His death an invaluable sum of merit into Father's hand for the good and use of all His people — unto eternity."

\* \* \* \*

## Divine Remembrance (Gen. 9: 15)

"When we read that God *remembers,* we are not to think for a moment that He at any time forgets — that is in its literal connotation. When He 'remembers' in the Biblical sense it means that He makes application of the Truth either in judgment or in mercy. When He 'remembers' our transgressions, our sins, He requires this at our hands. When He 'remembers' His 'covenant' on our behalf He forgives all."

\* \* \* \*

## Christ is All (Col. 3: 11)

"I am anxious to lay greater emphasis on the fact that Christ fulfilled the law in His life; so that the life He lived is the true pattern of the righteousness Adam was created in, but which he forfeited in his Fall; it is also the righteousness of the law and it is the righteousness of God inasmuch as He is God who brought it near; who preserved it; Who exalted it and made it honourable. And this righteousness answers to all God's demands and requirements; and this in turn answers to all man's requirements. Then there is the passive

126

obedience of Christ to be reckoned here; His satisfying divine justice, the full payment of the ransom. Here is where we must meet God in peace; these must be the terms of our reconciliation to God.''

* * *

## A Blessed Exchange

''I spent some of the night with Charnock. What fare is spread out on this table! And what spiritual digestion God imparted to those who made use of it in their time. 'He is said to be *made sin for us,* and we are said to be *made the righteousness of God in Him,* a blessed exchange for us'. 'How can that man take pleasure in anything he hath, when all the threatenings in the book of God are so many arrows directed against him?' And yet again, 'As a strong faith gives more glory to God, so it receives more comfort from Him'. God make me a power for good in our day and generation!''

* * * *

## A Balanced Theology

''I devoted the whole day to my studies. Reflected again on the dangers of Arminianism and of Antinomianism. It is essential to keep a balance here, and sound Calvinism is the only system that encourages this. John 11: 39: ''Loose him and let him go', verse 44; 'take away the stone', verse 39. Acts 3: 7; 28: 22-25, cp. 30-31: What fine balances in this area of doctrine and the application of doctrine do we find in John 11: 39, etc. How unlearned men confuse things that differ here! Our worthy fathers were men of the highest commonsense when they required of their ministers all the mental and academic equipment available in University and College for their holy and exacting work.''

* * * *

## The Spiritual Mind

''I prepared hard for the Monthly Meeting at 12 noon. Service was good. Text: 1 Cor. 11: 16. Described natural man as a man who lived on and by his senses — his fleshly appetites — just as the animals do. Things of the Spirit of God are folly to him. He cannot know them because they

127

K

are spiritually discerned. So he cannot know the mind of the Lord. But we have the mind of Christ. Confined this mind of Christ to the immediate context. Verse 12 explains this in terms of the things . . . freely given to us of God; verse 13 refers to this as comparing spiritual things with spiritual — these things freely given.''

*　　*　　*　　*

## An Ache for Repentance

''I have been out of my depth since Sabbath. God is displeased with me and I experience this in my soul. I see some glimmering of hope in the fact that I am thrown back on the simple, fundamental verities of the faith. *I have an ache for repentance towards God.* I am concerned as to the crucifying of the flesh, with the lusts thereof. But still I am conscious of His rebuke.''

*　　*　　*　　*

## God in Christ

''Studied all morning till 12 noon. Interested in Lk. 11: 14. Never in the history of world a wonder like this. Here we have God assuming human nature; the Creator of the ends of the earth becoming a creature; heaven entering into covenant with man — fallen man. Host of heaven sent at the birth of this prince. Augustus's Court were not in tune with this at all, but they had their very existence in virtue of all this. Angels appeared here at His incarnation; they ministered to Him after His temptation; then at His resurrection and at His ascension. And just as they ever attended on Him so they always wait on those that are His. They express their joy in praising — to speak in praise of — to praise — God. But He is not the Redeemer of Angels. 'To us a child is born'. They are pure from envy and pride. They praise Him for goodness poured out on us — inferior creatures to them.''

*　　*　　*　　*

''*They comparing themselves among themselves, are not wise — Lancashire Millworker.* Outside shop in his town there was a large clock. Every morning he set his watch by it. One day the owner of the clock said to him 'I see you always set your watch by my clock'. He replied 'that is so, I blow the

128

buzzer at the Mill and I must be sure to have the right time'. 'Well,' exclaimed the clock owner, 'if that doesn't beat the band — I have been setting my clock every day by your buzzer'.

There is but one perfect example — Jesus Christ. Let us be confronted to His likeness."

## The Blood on the Door-posts

"How solemn it is to tread this entrance into the New Year. My concern is to have the blood of Jesus Christ His Son on my lintel and on my two side posts. For the first time I was deeply movèd as I reflected on the part the door occupied in this great deliverance — this objective — this Godward aspect of their deliverance. The door was after all representative of the house, and the house comprehended all the individuals and affairs in it. Indeed the door was of the essence of things. Their very existence depended in all its majors on the doors. They could live without many things in the house, but the door entered into all their interest, their joys and sorrows, their safety and their all. This night of the passover was closely linked with their great deliverance at the Red Sea. Indeed the one was as much their exodus as the other. So in Christian experience, the appropriation of the blood of atonement is basic to peace, to the overthrow of His and our enemies. God be over, in, with, for and through us in the New Year!"

\*   \*   \*   \*

## God, our Home

"I made a visit to Neil's house, and was blessed in the prayer I had with them. I addressed God in the words of Ps. 90: 1-2. Then my mind in prayer reflected on the spirits made perfect in holiness and the heaven they enjoyed. Yes, they enjoyed heaven; they enjoyed the Lord in heaven; nay, the Lord was the heaven they enjoyed. That was how I conceived on my knees of Ps. 90: 'Thou has been our dwelling place' — that is in common parlance 'our home'."

\*   \*   \*   \*

## When Things appear to go Wrong

"Left at 9.20 a.m. for Benbecula en route to Inverness. Delayed at Benbecula until 5.00 p.m. Could not analyse this turn of events. But I had one special experience out of it. At 3.00 p.m. I made a long detour of part of the golf course there. Then I sat in a quiet section of it, took my hat off and had prayer. The Captain and Second Officer of a special plane that had landed earlier in the day, were having a walk along the shore at the time I was in my corner. On their way back they contacted me. A fine discussion started. After a while the Captain suggested we should have tea. During that whole time we discussed things at the highest levels of life and of death. I trust I shall meet them again.''

\* \* \* \*

**God, the sure Guide**

''In the course of my reading today, I landed on a sweet word from the mouth of the Lord. It was Ps. 107: 7. I got blessing from every word of it. In the course of my studies here I went back to a quotation the late dear Mr Macrae, Kinloch, often made: 'I am a stranger on this earth; hide not Thy laws from me'. He was anxious here, as David was, to have his course safely set for glory. So in the above text God guided in the straight way to the end, the city. It was a holy exercise.''

\* \* \* \*

**The Need for private Bible Study**

''Again and again God has rebuked me for not devoting more time to private reading of the Word, for my own personal benefit quite apart from my official work. God grant that if He spares me for another winter I shall not fail in this; that I shall set my face as a flint to the execution of this solemn essential requirement. The Lord encompassed me all day; no flesh could assail me.''

Our diarist, with his love of gardening, would have appreciated William Gurnall's metaphor where he writes, ''The saint is often compared to Christ's garden. There would not long hang any of their sweet fruit upon their souls were not Satan kept off with the point of this sword — the Word of God.''

Hence his emphasis on the private study of the Holy Scriptures.

# CHAPTER TWELVE

# THE END OF THE ROAD

**Death is the chariot sent for the believer's soul —
Resurrection the chariot sent for his body.**

—A. A. BONAR.

The Morrisons of Bayhead Manse began their last New Year together in their usual way. Let Mr Morrison tell us about it.

"1st January 1982: The Lord honoured us again in our waiting upon Him, as in previous years, on the threshold of the New Year. We sought His abundant care and rich mercy, as on bended knees we faced the New Year. We desired that the blood of Jesus Christ His Son should be on the lintel and on the two side-posts. Yes, and it was our desire and prayer that the Lord should add to our number in quality and in quantity; that all the good of the past years in our spirituals and in our temporals should continue to the end of time. It was late in the morning before we retired to rest. We had our prayer in a special way for the poor souls who are the slaves of strong drink. At the same time I feel that it is true to say this Island is not the worst by any means. On our way last night to conduct worship in the home of sorrow at Grimsay, there was hardly a car on the road. It was our prayer all along that the Lord should have His restraining grace in all this."

— 1 —

Although Mr Morrison had already come to the time of life that most men regard as appropriate to retirement, he was still, to all appearances, in full physical and mental vigour. If he at all spoke of retirement it was as an event for which he awaited direction from God. He was glad when the General Assembly passed legislation permitting ministers to retire at the age of 65 without having to submit a medical

131

certificate to the effect that they were no longer able to meet the full demands of their calling, but he regarded it as a minister's duty to continue in the yoke for as long as he could. There was the risk, as he would readily admit, that the minister himself might not be the best judge of the appropriate time for withdrawal, and he would express his own anxiety to know the mind of the Lord in the matter, lest by staying in harness, or putting it off too soon, he might prove a hindrance, and not a help, to the cause that he had so much at heart. He thought of Caleb.

"Worship had a message for me. We read in Joshua 13 and also in the New Testament. The word in Joshua 14 was made very precious to me. Caleb was 40 years old when he obtained the promise of an inheritance; but he was 85 years old before he obtained actual possession of his lot — the lot the Lord had decreed for him. The Lord, however, was not slow concerning His promise. He was sovereign in the matter and method of it all. This was a very precious word to me. My soul seems to cleave to the Lord for His help in all that He has committed to me not only for this day, but for the whole week also. I wait on God for *my* Hebron also."

He had not spared himself, and as he entered upon his seventies he was still hale and hearty. In a diary entry dated 10/1/71, he indeed makes passing mention of "something in the nature of a palpitation" that had kept him awake for part of the night before; and, later, there is more extended reference to a painful limp that he had developed. But there was nothing to cause alarm, and, after a brief slackening of pace, he was back to full duty. In the last year of his life, however, he seemed to have a premonition that the home-call was imminent.

On 11th January he wrote: "I'm beginning to note that my age is telling on me; in writing this I don't feel as steady as I used to. This should teach me to look to the Lord more consistently as my days go by."

And on 14th January 1982: "The Lord be pleased to direct my steps throughout the year; that is if it please Him to spare me for this year. This is the beginning of my 40th year in charge of this congregation. May it please the Lord to spare me, and to spare me in good health for a few years yet. The Lord knows that I have my enemies here; at the same time He knows that His enemies are my enemies also; yes, and His friends, I venture to think, are my friends also. We had an addition — a worthy addition — to our congregation here last year. May He grant us a greater addition this year both in quantity and quality. We had a sure token of love in the administration of our Sacraments last year and the Communion in November was specially blessed to us all. The Lord multiply such abundant mercies to us this coming year. We must also pray for the peace of God to guard our hearts in the fear of God. The Lord grant me ever to watch and pray.''

"15th January: I read the last chapter in Matthew. It touched me that the first verses of the chapter are related to, and speak of, the resurrection of the saints in terms of the Judgment Day. 'There was a great earthquake and the rocks did rend; and the graves were opened; and many bodies of the saints which slept arose and came out of the graves after His resurrection, and went into the holy city and appeared unto many.' The Lord grant that I should ever lay emphasis on the teaching of Phil. 1: 9 — that your 'love may abound more and more in all knowledge and in all judgment'. Unbelief makes the knowledge of spiritual things but as dreams though a man have much; whereas faith turns them all into realities and works upon the heart accordingly.

— 2 —

In February of that year he made what proved to be his last visit to Edinburgh, to attend a meeting of the Lord's Day Observance Society. In the course of the Executive meeting he intervened to suggest that perhaps our planning was in excess of our praying; and he proposed that we should break at this point for a word of prayer. The suggestion was heartily accepted, and the duty of leading in prayer was laid upon himself. He prayed as a man with a burden on his spirit, and yet in accents of conviction that the cause of Christ would yet be gloriously revived in Scotland, and a spiritually renewed Church would "look forth as the morning, fair as the moon, clear as the sun, and terrible as an army with banners''.

It was the last, but by no means the least, of his many public contributions to the work of the Society.

After the meeting, he sought out the present writer with the request that I should go to North Uist in June to assist him at the Grimsay Communion. At first I resisted, reminding him that I had been with him just two years ago, and suggested that my next visit might be postponed. But he was insistent.

"Do come, if it is at all possible for you," he urged. "I may be asking you for the last time."

In April he was at Bracadale, assisting his friend, Rev. Kenneth Mackay, at his communion services there. Throughout the weekend there was an unusually strong sense of the Divine Presence both in the Church services and in the Manse fellowship. Mr Morrison's branch throughout seemed heavy with heavenly dews, and his preaching brought blessing to many of his hearers.

"His wife also remarked," writes Rev. John Morrison, "that when he returned from that communion he was like one not altogether with us, but far above us. He told her that the sermon on Monday was a farewell sermon, and an omen that either Mr Mackay or himself was soon to pass away."

A day or two later a public transport bus from Glasgow to Uig, Skye, had a serious accident in which a young woman from Mr Morrison's congregation was badly injured. Her parents were gravely concerned, and their minister shared their concern. The prayer at family worship in the Manse that night gathered around the injured girl and her anxious parents. Before retiring for the night, Mr Morrison decided to ring up the hospital, in Inverness, to which she had been taken, to inquire as to her condition.

The report was reassuring. She was off the danger list, and was now progressing favourably. Mr Morrison decided not to go to bed until he had conveyed the good news to her parents, who were not on the phone. He walked briskly, and on arriving, he was perspiring; so, after having given his good tidings, he sat resting awhile, chatting with the family, before setting out for home. But James Morrison had taken his last walk. Within a few minutes he was dead. Donald Archie Mackay's house at Balemore became the scene of his departure for the Father's House in glory.

It was a fitting close to a faithful and caring ministry. Only a few months before he had written, "I am at one with Toplady when he wrote 'I would rather die in harness than in the stall'."

He had his wish.

— 3 —

Mr Morrison's funeral brought together a large concourse of mourners. They were there from Lewis, Harris, Skye, North Uist, South Uist, as well as from various parts of the mainland. Former associates in the work of local government — including his friend, Earl Granville — came to pay their last tribute to his memory. The service in the Church was conducted by Rev. Allan Macleod, of Sleat Free Church, as Moderator of the local Presbytery, and the praise was led by Mr Morrison's missionary-assistant, Mr Bannatyne Macleod, whose regard for his minister was so fully reciprocated. Thence the cortege made their way to the cemetery of Kilmuir, on the west side of North Uist, where devout men carried him from the hearse to the last resting place which had been prepared for him there in accordance with his own wish. Rev. John Morrison offered prayer at the grave. And there, with the background sough of the Atlantic mingling with their supplications, they left him "till the day break and the shadows flee away".

In a presbyterial tribute, contributed to the *Free Church Monthly Record,* the Rev. Donald MacDonald of Carloway, says: "On the day of the funeral, the small beautiful Paible church, which was so dear to Mr Morrison's heart and on which he had expended much time and labour in order to bring it to the fine state of repair in which it now stands, was filled to capacity with people from all over and outwith the island and from every denomination — an indication of the high esteem in which Mr Morrison was

135

justly held. Members from the Skye and Lewis Presbyteries conducted the funeral service, after which the mortal remains were interred in the very soil he so dearly loved, there to await the morning of the Resurrection of the righteous. The large concourse of mourners who witnessed the interment seemed reluctant to leave the scene, finding it so difficult to realise that this faithful servant of Christ was forever removed from their midst.

'Well done thou good and faithful servant, enter thou into the joy of thy Lord.'

The sorrowing congregation paid their silent tribute to his memory in the words which they caused to be inscribed on the memorial stone which marks his last resting place — beginning and ending it in his mother-tongue which he loved so dearly.

MAR CHUIMHNEACHAN
AIR AN URR SEUMAS MOIREASDAN
DE MHUNNTIR SCALPAIGH NA HEARADH
AGUS A CHAOCHAIL AN UIBHIST A TUATH
AIR AN 9MH DHEN GIBLEAN 1982
IS E 72 BLIADHNA DH'AOIS
ERECTED
BY THE FREE CHURCH CONGREGATIONS
OF NORTH UIST AND GRIMSAY
IN LOVING MEMORY OF
REV. JAMES MORRISON M.A.
THEIR PASTOR FROM 1942 TO 1982
AN ABLE MINISTER OF THE WORD
LUCID IN EXPOSITION
STRONG IN CONVICTION
COURAGEOUS IN WITNESS TO THE TRUTH
A LOVING HUSBAND
A FAITHFUL PASTOR
A LOYAL FRIEND

"GUS AM BRIS AN LA AGUS AN TEICH NA SGAILEAN"
DAN SHOL :17

\*　　\*　　\*　　\*

It is a tribute to Mr Morrison's influence over young people that a young islesman* with bardic gifts, and a mystic turn of mind, wrote some verses about him entitled *The Root from the Corn* in which the following words occur:

> But though I cannot say I knew you well
> I need not know the flower's name to see the hue;
> I've seen earth's television shake in prayer,
> And say no man on earth impressed me more than you.

\* \* \* \*

> After here, and setting of the sun,
> The new day's snares will keener be I know,
> The rivers all flow downward to the seas,
> But seas can never tell us when they're full.

\* \* \* \*

> O'er pastel machairs, winds smell sweet and blow,
> The wild birds learn on Uist's gentle greens
> The poppy scatters lazy through the corn
> We turn for home to wrestle with our years.

— 4 —

When I went to Grimsay in June, in accordance with my promise to him, I found a subdued people mourning a pastor whose true worth, as many of them were ready to admit, they had never fully realised until he was taken from them. James Morrison's most enduring memorial in North Uist is not to consist in the improved communications that he helped to procure for the people, nor the local industries that he helped to foster, nor any other benefits which may have accrued to the Western Isles from his advocacy of their cause as the elected representative of the people. Rather, it will be found in the changed lives of men and women whom he taught to seek first the kingdom of God and His righteousness, and to expect from God both that

* Calum MacDonald, the song-writer of *Runrig* — a group that has performed before audiences in Europe and Australia, as well as throughout Great Britain.

and the addition of the "other things" in such measure as it might please Him to bestow them.

An ardent admirer of Dr James Begg, Mr Morrison contended for the very things that Begg upheld a century before — the inerrancy of Holy Scripture, the abiding authority of the Fourth Commandment, and the defence of our Protestantism against the assaults of Romanism. And, to quote from Robertson Nicoll's appreciation of Dr Begg, "are not the Bible and the Sabbath what he called them — the two great pillars of visible religion? Has ever religion flourished where the Book and the Day have been despised? And when all is said and done, is not Roman Catholicism a standing menace to our country?"

Such "lost causes", as some deem them, have always shown an extraordinary capacity of revival, and will continue to do so, because God is in them.

"My own hope is" wrote Robert Browning,

> "a sun will pierce
> the thickest cloud earth ever stretched;
> That after Last returns the First,
> though a wide compass round be fetched;
> That what began best can't end worst,
> Nor what God blessed once prove accurst."

That was James Morrison's hope too, and it was the inspiration of his whole ministry, yes to the very end. For he was near the end when he recorded the following cry from the heart in his diary:

I have still a pain in my heart for my poor parishioners. O Lord, come, come, come and save them.

*(The following Gaelic elegy on Mr Morrison was composed, shortly after his death, by the Lewis bard, Kenneth John Smith, and is reproduced here from his recent book* Rùn mo Smuaintean, *by his kind permission.*

*Mr Smith refers to the fact that the last communion services at which Mr Morrison assisted in Lewis were those held in Berneray in September 1981.)*

## MAR CHIUMHNEACHAN AIR AN URRAMACH SEUMAS MOIREASDAN NACH MAIREANN, A BHA ANN AN UIBHIST

Gu'n cuala mi sgeul a chuir mulad am chre
Mu'n teachdaire threun a bu ghrasmhoir
A bha ann an Uibhist is beathachadh treud
Is e labhairt riu sgeulachd na slainte.

Bha uallach an treid a riamh ann ad chre
'S tu toirt cruithneachd 'o d' bheul gach trath dhaibh,
'S am mana tha falaicht' 's tha tighinn bho neamh
Dhoibh chuir thu an ceill gu slainteil.

Cha tugadh tu gnuis do nithean gun luths—
'S tu dheanadh na cuisean ud aireamh;
'S a chruithneachd gun togadh tu gu fiorghlan is dluth
'S am moll gun cuireadh fo d' shail e.

Mar fhear-glanaidh 'is fasgnaidh bha thu eudmhor a riamh
Agus fiamh cha robh 'n ad do phairtean,
'S gach ni nach biodh fallain, a riamh b' e do mhiann
A thogail bho 'fhreumhan as aite.

'S ann an Sgalpaigh na Hearadh a thogadh tu suas
'Measg sluaigh a bha uasal 'is grasmhor,
'S an co-chomann bha agad 'o d' oige fo'm buaidh
Gun do chum e thu suas 's cha do dh'fhailing.

Measg chleachdaidhean fallainn bha againn 'n ar linn
Tha an canain a bha binn do gach mathair—
A Ghaidlig bha cridheil a riamh chum thu suas
'S gu robh i leat measail is sar-ghlan.

\*'N uair a thainig thu thugainn a chuideachadh leinn
Aig am co-chruinneachaidh grasmhor,
Air ordugh an Fhoghair, bha thu fior-ghlan is grinn
Toirt dhuinn mar dheanadh do lamhan.

'N uair 'fhritheal thu 'm bord mar Shoisgealach coir
'S tu 'labhairt mu dhoigh na slainte,
Gun d'shileadh na deoir fo bhriathrean do bheoil
'S bha spiorad bho Ghloir an lathair.

Ach a nis tha thu shuas an co-chomann an Uain
'S tu seinn le fior bhuaidh air do chlarsaich,
'S do ghrian bidh gu buan a dealradh le buaidh
Is pailm a tha nuadh 'na do lamhan.

Tha mi 'guidh gu caomh air a son-sa bha dluth,
'S a tha nise 'n a h-aonar 's an fhasach,
'S do d' chairdean tha le muirn 'g ad ionndrainn mar aon
'S an suil ri Ceannard na Slainte.

Tha am fasach a th'ann 'dol na fhasalachd dhuinn,
'S na solais a fas gann ann an aireamh;
'S tha 'n corran gach am toirt air falbh na naoimh ann,
'S cha chluinn sinn neach tighinn nan aite.

Nach math gu'm bheil comharr' ri fhaicinn 's an treud
'S gum bheil seulachainn orra bho'n airde
'S a dh'aindheoin galar is trioblaid bhios aca 'n an cre'
Tre ghealladh Mhic Dhe tha iad sabhailt'.

Bho nach bard mi gu labhairt air nithean tha mor
Nach tuigear air doigh ach am pairtean,
'S e mo ghuidhe gun tigeadh oirnn oiteag 'o Ghloir
A thogadh gu beo 'o n'a bhas sinn.

\* (S iad orduighean an fhoghair ann am Bearnaraigh na h-orduighean mu
dheireadh a fhritheil Mgr Moireasdan an Leodhas.)

The Last Resting Place *(see page 136).*